Input/Output

TIME® LIFE BOOKS

Other Publications:
YOUR HOME
THE ENCHANTED WORLD
THE KODAK LIBRARY OF CREATIVE PHOTOGRAPHY
GREAT MEALS IN MINUTES
THE CIVIL WAR
PLANET EARTH
COLLECTOR'S LIBRARY OF THE CIVIL WAR
THE EPIC OF FLIGHT
THE GOOD COOK
WORLD WAR II
HOME REPAIR AND IMPROVEMENT
THE OLD WEST

This volume is one of a series that examines
various aspects of computer technology and the
role computers play in modern life.

COVER

The essential job of input/output technology is
to take in raw data for processing by a computer and send it out as useful information, as in
this artistic conception of a plotter drawing
a color-coded map based on real-world information translated into digital signals.

UNDERSTANDING COMPUTERS

Input/Output

BY THE EDITORS OF TIME-LIFE BOOKS
TIME-LIFE BOOKS, ALEXANDRIA, VIRGINIA

Contents

7   Flexible Systems for a World of Information
ESSAY   Charting the Path of Input/Output

     1

35   Evolving from Number Cruncher
to Word Machine
ESSAY   Team Players for Instant Interaction

     2

61   En Route to Compatible Computing

     3

77   Of Medicine, Machines and Other Marvels
ESSAY   Flying with the Ultimate Copilot

     4

95   Transcending Limitations and Boundaries
ESSAY   A New Definition of Control in Music and Sound

     5

122   Glossary
123   Bibliography
125   Acknowledgments, Picture Credits
126   Index

Flexible Systems for a World of Information

In a fitting clash of old and new, a traditional brass band played patriotic tunes, then throbbing electronic music enlivened a modernistic light show as the Grumman Aerospace Corporation proudly unveiled its experimental X-29 fighter plane at Calverton, Long Island, in the summer of 1984. The featured speaker, Vice President George Bush — a former U.S. Navy flier — gazed at the new aircraft and quipped to the audience, "That's a beautiful model, but they've got the wings on backward."

The X-29 did indeed appear to have been assembled in reverse. The wings of most planes angle back toward the tail, but the X-29 had wings that swept disconcertingly forward. Grumman's design, however, was no mistake. Engineers long had been aware of the aerodynamic advantages offered by forward-sweeping wings. Among them are improved lift, reduced drag, freedom from the threat of stalling during steep climbs and the ability to make sharp turns at more than the speed of sound. Until recently, however, two obstacles prevented the aviation industry from putting forward-swept-wing theories into practice with supersonic aircraft. The materials used to construct conventional airplane wings were either too weak or too heavy to sustain the forward-swept design, and the inherent instability of such a plane was more than ordinary guidance equipment could cope with.

The first problem was solved by the development of a reinforced, lightweight composite material for the wings. The second challenge — controlling the skittish plane in flight — was solved by advances in computer technology. The X-29 is, in effect, an airborne research laboratory for forward-swept wings, notable not so much for its onboard computers as for the peripheral input and output devices that constantly enter critical flight data into the computers and instantly retrieve the resulting information for action — adjusting the control surfaces many times a second so that the plane does not tear itself to pieces in midair (pages 85-93).

Input/output, or I/O, technology is the practical adjunct to computer science. Its roots reach further back than those of computers themselves, and its development has challenged the best minds of the computer age. The scientists' and engineers' hard-won success in answering two mundane questions — how to put data and instructions into a computer and how to get the processed information out in useful form — has resulted in a wealth of hardware and software solutions. These innovations have expanded the versatility of computer use to the borders of human imagination, from the detailed design of artificial bones to the playing of music without musicians, or the flying of an "unflyable" aircraft.

Over the years, engineering and programming creativity has made it possible for computer users to put information into the machine by such varied means as

Punched tape (top), binary numbers (right) and digitized graphics merge seamlessly in the single surface of a Möbius strip, representing three of the many forms the same information may take as it enters and leaves a computer.

flipping switches on a control panel, manipulating plugs, typing on a keyboard or a numeric key pad, drawing with a stylus on an electronic tablet, speaking into a microphone or touching a fingertip to a display screen. In many cases, computers can receive input from other machines without human intervention. Weather satellites, for example, beam information to earthbound computers that render the signals into spectacular color photographs.

Output technology also is marvelously varied. Some early computers displayed their results by causing lights to go on or off in particular patterns; such output systems required specialized knowledge to decipher the meaning of the lights, and they quickly gave way to more understandable, or "user-friendly," alternatives. Some output devices, such as cathode-ray tubes (CRTs), are best suited for presenting ephemeral, or rapidly changing, output; they are preferred, for example, for the viewing of text that is still in the process of being composed or edited. When a document is finished, other devices, such as computer-controlled printers, provide a so-called hard copy—a permanent type of output. Computers can produce output in the form of artificial voices or other sound effects, played through a speaker system. In certain instances, when a computer does not have to communicate with a human user, it can address its output to another machine in the form of electronic signals. The X-29 is a case in point: a machine essentially guided by electronic computer output.

In recent years, I/O technology at times has seemed to overshadow computer science itself; I/O equipment is more varied, frequently more expensive and may require more space than the computer it serves. I/O equipment also has developed a speed of delivery that almost matches a main processor's lightning-fast capacity for calculation. Such, however, was not always the case.

MAKESHIFT MEANS OF COMMUNICATION

Many of the devices first used for computer input and output predated computers themselves; they were simply grafted onto the computer when the need arose. Often the result was a jury-rigged system in which the I/O equipment was neither convenient for the user nor sufficiently well matched to the computer to take full advantage of the machine's capacities. Until the advent of standardization, each piece of I/O equipment required its own coding system and specially designed hardware and software for transferring coded information into the computer and getting processed results back out. But the main handicap of these adapted devices was a frustrating lack of speed. It did little good for the computer to be capable of thousands of calculations per second if the input and output took minutes, hours or even days.

The most important of the borrowed devices was the punched card, a concept that can be traced to 18th-century attempts to automate the silk-weaving industry. By 1804, a Frenchman, Joseph Marie Jacquard, had introduced a mechanical loom controlled by sequences of punched cards. The placement of the holes in the cards dictated the pattern in the cloth by governing the movement of individual throws of the shuttle.

Later in the 19th century, the English mathematical genius Charles Babbage and his collaborator Augusta Ada Byron, the Countess of Lovelace, seized on Jacquard's punched cards as a means of programming a mammoth steam-driven machine called the Analytical Engine. The Analytical Engine was a brilliant dream; it sought to do with meshing gears what computers of a future age would accomplish with relay switches, vacuum tubes and silicon micro-circuits. But Babbage and Lovelace were trapped in the wrong century; the giant mechanical computer was only partially built. Its punched-card input system, however, eventually would be embraced by the world's business community in many ways.

The modern father of the computer punched card was the American inventor and entrepreneur Herman Hollerith. In 1890, Hollerith, the son of German immigrants, undertook the task of mechanizing the processing of the United States census. He devised a punched-card tabulating system that counted and categorized the nation's expanding population three times as fast as an army of human clerks had been able to do the job 10 years earlier. As a contemporary said, it got out the result "while it was still interesting."

Following Hollerith's triumph with the census, tabulators using punched cards for input emerged as a major tool of American business. Hollerith himself founded the Tabulating Machine Company, which later merged with several other firms to evolve into the International Business Machines Corporation—the future goliath of the computer industry. Through the first half of the 20th century, IBM and its competitors profited handsomely from the business world's increasing reliance on machines for counting and calculating. By the 1930s, automatic tabulating had advanced to the point where a Pittsburgh department store could install a system in which 250 terminals throughout the store were connected by telephone lines to a central bank of tabulators. Goods were priced with punched tags, and the information on the tags was transmitted automatically to the tabulators; they recorded the sale and returned to the customer an invoice that was typed out at the terminal by an automatic typewriter.

By the dawn of the computer age, in the 1940s, many engineers who were otherwise remarkably inventive deemed it practical to continue using punched cards simply because they were a proven entity—and because the conservative giant IBM was deeply committed to them. Physically, the card had become a rectangle that was stiffer than a sheet of writing paper but thinner and more flexible than a shirt cardboard. As in Hollerith's original system, information was punched into the card in rows and columns of small holes (the card often bore a printed warning to the user not to "fold, spindle or mutilate" lest the data on it be destroyed).

Typically, cards were fed into a computer in batches of several hundred at a time, just as they had been fed into mechanical tabulators. A reading device similar to one developed by Hollerith inspected each card by laying it flat on a metal plate and brushing it with a set of delicate wire sensors. The wires sensed nothing when they brushed the surface of the card, but at each hole they made contact with the metal beneath the card, completing an electrical connection. The computer read each contact as a fragment of data. A separate device called a verifier checked the accuracy of the punch operator's work, and when a card became worn, a reproducing punch replaced it with a new one.

Since the computer could produce useful results only if it received each batch of input in precisely the right sequence, the system provided abundant opportunities for error. The unfortunate operator who dropped and scattered a box of punched cards would cause general dismay and bring a computer project to a standstill. (Fortunately, sequence numbers were put on the back of each card to facilitate getting the cards back in the right order.)

An early alternative to punched cards as an input/output medium was perforated paper tape, which had the advantage of recording data on continuous strips rather than on batches of individual cards. Paper tape's precomputer origins can be traced to the moving strips of paper used in 19th-century telegraph receivers and—a little later in its genealogy—to the teletypewriter, a machine introduced in Chicago early in the 20th century by the father-son engineering team of Charles and Howard Krum. Their invention, which involved punched holes in rolls of paper tape and synchronized keyboards that printed out messages in typescript, wrought a revolution in telegraphic communication, which until then had generally required skilled key operators at either end of a line transmitting messages by Samuel Morse's code of dots and dashes.

As adapted to tabulators and later to experimental computers, the perforated paper tape served the same purpose as punched cards and was read by similar sensing devices. Usually, after a tape was punched, its ends were glued together to form a paper loop. Subroutines—small programs embedded within larger

Data Processing's Durable Workhorse

Once the primary means of computer input, punched cards have remained basically unchanged since Herman Hollerith designed them for tabulating the 1890 census. A modern card *(below)*—closely modeled on a version introduced by IBM in 1928—has a clipped upper right-hand corner to keep data processors from stacking it upside down or backward. Numbers, letters and symbols are punched in the card's 80 vertical columns according to a variation of the code Hollerith devised: A number is encoded by a single hole in one of the lower nine horizontal rows, a letter by two holes—one in a so-called numeric row, the other in one of the three classifying "zone" rows at the top—and symbols by two or more holes.

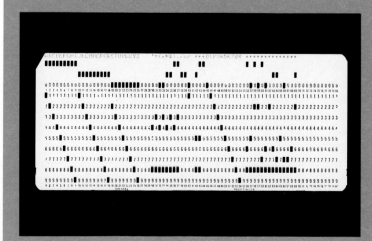

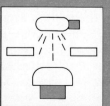

Two of the most common methods of converting information punched on cards into electronic pulses for a digital computer are illustrated at left. The electromechanical technique *(top)* sandwiches the card between a metal roller and a row of 80 small metal brushes, one brush for each column on the card. When a brush dips into a hole, it touches the roller, closing an electrical circuit and sending a signal to the computer. With the second type of card reader *(bottom)*, tiny photoelectric cells sense beams of light passing through the holes.

programs—could be coded on separate loops and threaded into separate readers. This saved the computer time by giving it the swiftest possible access to each set of instructions. But paper tape had an obvious handicap: its vulnerability to tearing. A torn tape could be as much of a disaster as a spilled batch of punched cards. To avoid tearing, the tape had to be pulled slowly through the reader with only moderate stress, and this naturally frustrated users who wanted maximum speed from their I/O devices.

Computer pioneer George Stibitz of Bell Laboratories employed paper tape in the seminal Complex Number Calculator, which he developed shortly before World War II. Stibitz's machine, eventually known as the Model I, was built around the on-off relay switches that Bell Labs had been using since the 1920s to process dialed numbers and to control the routing of telephone calls. Stibitz set out to solve mathematical problems with sequences of relays that operated according to the binary system, which represents all numbers as strings of the digits one and zero. With the on and off positions of the switches symbolizing ones and zeros respectively, Stibitz designed his machine to carry out calculations by opening and closing the switches at high speed. A user could enter two eight-digit numbers through a teletypewriter keyboard, instruct the Complex Number Calculator to divide one number into the other and see the answer clatter out on the same teletypewriter within 30 seconds.

World War II provided an atmosphere of urgency—and an outpouring of government funds—that stimulated the infant computer science to grow in many exciting directions. But input/output technology continued to rely on the tried and true, as exemplified by British efforts to decipher coded German radio traffic. Scientists assigned to the top-secret *Ultra* project constructed a series of room-size machines in which the electromechanical relays used by Stibitz and others were replaced by vacuum tubes; yet the intercepted enemy messages were fed into Colossus, as machines in this series were called, in the familiar way—as symbols punched into a loop of paper tape. Colossus was a successful project, but it was not without hazard. Not only was the paper tape susceptible to tearing but at high speeds (Colossus was capable of scanning 5,000 characters per second) the exposed edge of the paper had the cutting potential of a buzz saw.

THE IMPETUS OF GUNNERY CONTROL
In the United States during this period, computer development was spurred by the need for quick answers to problems of artillery ballistics. Because tape readers were used to control some of the most advanced artillery systems of the day, a computer could design a series of test instructions for firing a new weapon and produce the test results on a perforated paper tape; the tape then became input for the weapon's control system.

A landmark machine begun during the war, ENIAC, for Electronic Numerical Integrator and Computer, could calculate the trajectory of a shell faster than the shell itself could travel from gun muzzle to target. ENIAC, developed for the army at the University of Pennsylvania's Moore School of Engineering, pushed the use of vacuum tubes to new levels of efficiency, but it made do with an I/O system that worked at a crawl compared with the computer itself. It used punched cards for input, and it was manually programmed: Before the computer could begin solving mathematical problems at dazzling speed, technicians spent hours setting switches by hand and plugging cables into sockets one at a time to interconnect the various parts of the system.

The freshets of change that would ultimately transform input/output equipment were most evident in another war-inspired computer, appropriately dubbed Whirlwind—this one at the Massachusetts Institute of Technology. In 1944, the U.S. Navy commissioned a team of M.I.T. engineers headed by Jay W. Forrester to develop a computer that would solve problems of aircraft stability and control in a new flight simulator. The result was a monster, filling a two-story building from basement to roof, that took six years to become operational. By then, the navy had lost interest, and Whirlwind's funding had been taken over by the newly independent U.S. Air Force, which was desperately trying to modernize its air-defense system for the continental United States. Whirlwind gave early use to two I/O devices adapted from other technologies, the cathode-ray tube (CRT) and the Flexowriter.

The CRT that Whirlwind employed to display its output was similar to a television monitor, consisting of a large vacuum tube in which streams of electrons lighted up a phosphor-coated screen. For a more permanent record, infor-

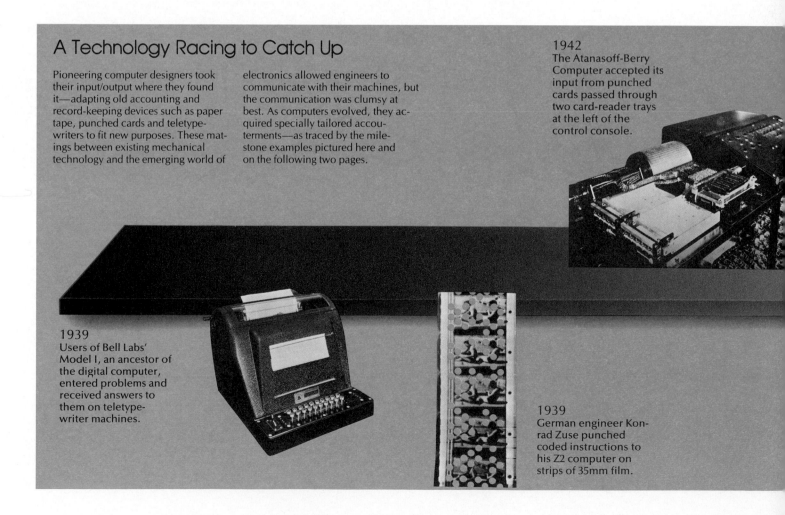

A Technology Racing to Catch Up

Pioneering computer designers took their input/output where they found it—adapting old accounting and record-keeping devices such as paper tape, punched cards and teletypewriters to fit new purposes. These matings between existing mechanical technology and the emerging world of electronics allowed engineers to communicate with their machines, but the communication was clumsy at best. As computers evolved, they acquired specially tailored accouterments—as traced by the milestone examples pictured here and on the following two pages.

1942
The Atanasoff-Berry Computer accepted its input from punched cards passed through two card-reader trays at the left of the control console.

1939
Users of Bell Labs' Model I, an ancestor of the digital computer, entered problems and received answers to them on teletypewriter machines.

1939
German engineer Konrad Zuse punched coded instructions to his Z2 computer on strips of 35mm film.

mation could be printed on a typewriter-like machine—the Flexowriter. A descendant of the old player piano and the teletypewriter, the Flexowriter had the dual capacity to print out words and punch coded holes in paper tape. It was the primitive ancestor of an I/O machine as yet barely dreamed of: the word processor.

In the 1950s, Whirlwind became the prototype for a series of computers that enabled the air force to build a sophisticated air defense called the SAGE, or Semi-Automatic Ground Environment, system. SAGE was capable of handling simultaneous input from 23 regional centers in the United States and Canada that monitored an enormous network of radar installations and other sensors. Operators at each center typed data on input keyboards and watched circular display screens to keep track of weather conditions, aircraft flight patterns and other information essential to air defense. At the same time, SAGE's battery of I/O devices, using telephone lines to send and receive signals, maintained communication between adjacent centers, knitting the entire system into a seamless whole. The original Whirlwind was retired from service at M.I.T. in 1959, but some of its direct successors were still in operation in the mid-1980s.

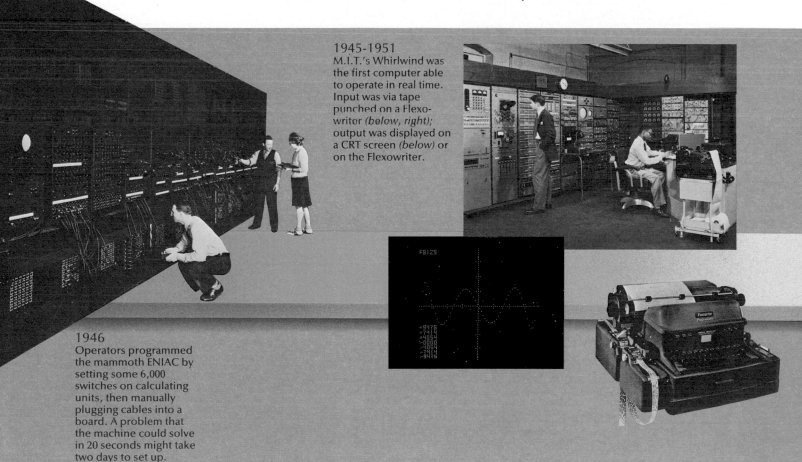

1945-1951
M.I.T.'s Whirlwind was the first computer able to operate in real time. Input was via tape punched on a Flexowriter (below, right); output was displayed on a CRT screen (below) or on the Flexowriter.

1946
Operators programmed the mammoth ENIAC by setting some 6,000 switches on calculating units, then manually plugging cables into a board. A problem that the machine could solve in 20 seconds might take two days to set up.

The creative ferment spawned by World War II continued to bubble on both sides of the Atlantic after the fighting stopped. In Great Britain, a Cambridge University team headed by Maurice Wilkes in 1949 unveiled the world's first large-scale computer designed to store its own programs. Input to the new machine, which was called EDSAC, or Electronic Delay Storage Automatic Calculator, was by paper tape.

Wilkes had spent the war years working on military radar, a field in which Great Britain led the world. As it happened, the most important postwar application of radar technology to computers came from another British researcher, F. C. Williams. Williams had labored during the war on a method of displaying radar data on a CRT, and in the late 1940s, he became part of a team at the University of Manchester building a computer called the Manchester Mark I. He brought his wartime dream to fruition with a new output device, a series of screens on which data in the computer's memory could be viewed and altered as the machine worked on a program.

One visiting programmer soon put Williams' invention to novel use by writing a program that played checkers, displaying the board and pieces on

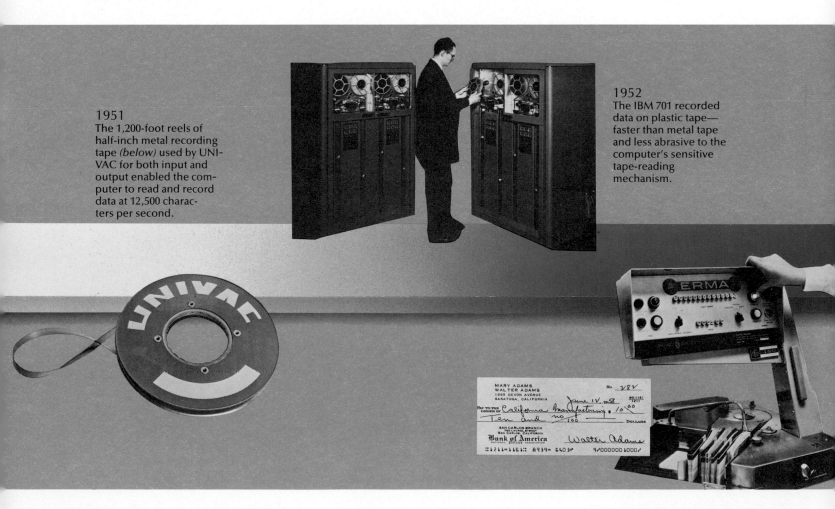

1951
The 1,200-foot reels of half-inch metal recording tape (below) used by UNI-VAC for both input and output enabled the computer to read and record data at 12,500 characters per second.

1952
The IBM 701 recorded data on plastic tape—faster than metal tape and less abrasive to the computer's sensitive tape-reading mechanism.

the Manchester Mark I's screen. The checkers program generated aural as well as visual output, playing "God Save the King" over a loudspeaker at the conclusion of the game.

The application was frivolous, but the input/output techniques it employed represented serious advances. In addition to displaying data on its CRT, the Manchester Mark I could produce information in the form of punched paper tape or text printed by teleprinter. It could accept both direct keyboard strokes and paper-tape input. The computer and its I/O equipment constituted a system that was a challenge to operate, however. Parts of the system were housed on separate floors, so that users had to scurry up and down a flight of stairs, setting switches by hand in one place, loading paper tape in another, and hoping all the while that the cars and lorries jouncing by on the street outside would not undo their delicate work.

In the United States, physicist John W. Mauchly and electrical engineer J. Presper Eckert, prime movers of the team that had built ENIAC at the University of Pennsylvania, were working on a more advanced model called EDVAC, or Electronic Discrete Variable Computer, when the war ended. More compact and

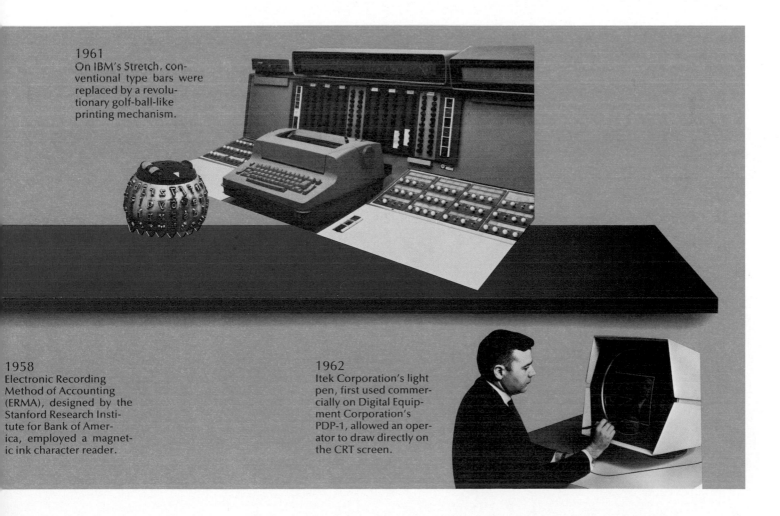

1961
On IBM's Stretch, conventional type bars were replaced by a revolutionary golf-ball-like printing mechanism.

1958
Electronic Recording Method of Accounting (ERMA), designed by the Stanford Research Institute for Bank of America, employed a magnetic ink character reader.

1962
Itek Corporation's light pen, first used commercially on Digital Equipment Corporation's PDP-1, allowed an operator to draw directly on the CRT screen.

yet more powerful than ENIAC, the new machine reduced the amount of manual plug and switch work needed to prepare it for each new program. Mauchly and Eckert left the university in 1946 to go into business for themselves, hoping to sell general-purpose computers to corporate as well as government clients. Although they met with disappointments as businessmen, they continued to show brilliance in science, developing two systems of lasting importance to the evolution of I/O technology.

One system, completed in 1949, was called BINAC, for Binary Automatic Computer. Designed for the Northrop Aircraft Company, it was small enough (five by four by one foot) to be operated inside an airplane in flight. BINAC could receive data from a typewriter keyboard or from encoded magnetic tape. Magnetic tape, which had been used in some calculators before the advent of the computer, operated on a principle similar to that of the newly popular tape recorder: Its slender plastic ribbon was specially coated to store data as magnetic fields induced by electric signals. Like the reels of ribbon on a recorder, the tape was erasable and could be used again and again.

For a variety of reasons, BINAC never operated properly, but Eckert and Mauchly were already working on a more ambitious machine called UNIVAC, or Universal Automatic Computer. This system was completed in 1951 and marketed soon thereafter by Remington Rand, a major manufacturer of punched-card tabulators, which had acquired Mauchly and Eckert's financially sagging firm.

UNIVAC was the first computer in the United States built for commercial applications, and it was successful in part because of the I/O components it offered. Eckert and Mauchly had set out to develop a magnetic tape for UNIVAC that could be used for both input and output. Unlike the rather flimsy plastic tape employed by BINAC, the UNIVAC tape was metallic. Moreover, it was compact. A single reel could hold 1,200 feet of the half-inch-wide tape, and one inch of tape could store 100 or more decimal digits. Thus, one reel could store more than a million characters of data, the equivalent of tens of thousands of cards.

The Eckert-Mauchly team built an electronic reader called the UNISERVO that transferred data to and from the tape at speeds that promised to revolutionize input/output processing. UNISERVO could read 12,500 characters per second, but the metal tape proved too wearing on the sensitive heads of the high-speed reader, and in subsequent designs, metal was abandoned in favor of new plastic compounds that were durable but less abrasive.

THE BIRTH OF HIGH-SPEED PRINTING
Perhaps the most successful component in UNIVAC's family of I/O devices was its high-speed printer. The need for such a printer had been evident from the start, if businesses were to make effective use of their computers for payroll, billing and inventory control. Some promising technology already existed. A machine retrieved from a captured German submarine during the war had included a curious "on-the-fly" printer in which hammers drove paper against a continuously rotating type wheel. Several American firms were experimenting with ways to improve this concept when the UNIVAC team decided to build a printer of its own.

The assignment fell to a project manager named Earl Masterson, and the instrument he designed in conjunction with J. Presper Eckert became the world's first commercially viable high-speed printer. Years later, Masterson recalled that the impetus to build the printer had come from Remington Rand's marketing department. "Marketing could not find another customer to buy the UNIVAC unless it was capable of producing great volumes of output. The pressure on us to get the printer finished was ungodly."

When the first UNIVAC was delivered—to the U.S. Census Bureau, in 1951—Masterson was still working on a prototype of his invention. But by 1954, he had finished a machine whose principles would become a permanent part of I/O technology. Called UNIPRINTER, Masterson's creation was a line printer: It was capable of printing an entire line of 120 characters virtually simultaneously, instead of typing one character at a time, as printers had done since the introduction of the typewriter in the 19th century.

The ingenious piece of equipment that made line printing possible and practical was a rotating drum. Embossed on the drum was a series of complete sets of type characters—one set circling the drum for each of the 120 print positions on a line. A hammer at each print position struck paper and ribbon, pushing them against the appropriate character as the drum spun rapidly on its horizontal axis. Driven by vacuum tubes that required 14,000 watts of power, Masterson's printer received reels of magnetic tape containing information processed by the central computer and printed the data out at a rate of 600 lines per minute, four times faster than its closest competition, the tabulators being used as printers by IBM.

In all, 46 UNIVAC Model I's were sold to government and commercial customers during the 1950s, and although the high-speed printer was sold as an optional extra, Masterson could recall proudly that "almost everyone who bought the computer also bought the printer."

IBM ENTERS THE FRAY
Like a languid giant resting with one eye prudently open, the International Business Machines Corporation watched the progress of computer science and input/output technology for a time without seeming to bestir itself. IBM may have recognized that once the development work was done by others, the firm could retain its hard-won position as kingpin of the office-machine industry simply by adapting the new equipment to its own profitable line of punched-card calculators. Or perhaps IBM feared running afoul of antitrust regulations if it moved too soon to exploit the computer field.

For whatever reason, IBM undertook no new work on computers in the immediate postwar years, even though it had earlier been a partner in computer research at Harvard and M.I.T. What is more, the company turned down the opportunity to buy up Mauchly and Eckert's firm before the struggling scientists turned to Remington Rand. IBM's conservative reputation was such that one scientist who was leaving his government job to go to work for IBM was warned by his colleagues, "That punched-card company will never produce a computer."

Few prophecies, of course, have been further from the mark. All along, there was stirring behind the scenes at IBM, and in a curious way it was research into input/output technology that eventually roused the company. IBM engineers had been badgering management to renew its interest in the incipient computer revolution, and they found a listener in Thomas J. Watson Jr., executive vice president and son of the chairman of the board. The junior Watson, a pilot in World War II, had been deeply impressed by the advanced radar and other military technology he encountered while in uniform, and he evidently used his considerable influence to move the company toward adapting the latest electronic techniques.

By 1949, IBM's management had approved a study of magnetic tape, to determine how much of a threat the new medium posed to the office-equipment systems that were IBM's bread and butter. Some of the corporation's executives doubted that magnetic tape ever would be a significant force in the business-machine market; unlike punched cards, which could be checked manually, magnetic tape required special machinery to check for errors. Moreover, IBM had a vast investment—and held most of the patents—in punched-card technology. But the study went forward, and in building machines to test the capabilities of magnetic tape, IBM engineers laid the foundation for the company's computer business.

A PROGENITOR SYSTEM
In 1952, IBM introduced its first fully electronic computer, originally called the Defense Calculator and later the 701. Although the new machine continued to use punched cards, it was supported by an array of advanced I/O technology, including CRTs, high-speed line printers and magnetic tape made of plastic. The Model 702, which soon followed and was created for commercial use, offered the customer the choice of reading information into the machine from cards or from magnetic tape, and of delivering output to tape or to a paper printer. By the mid-1950s, IBM engineers were developing a magnetic disk for storing information and a device called a data synchronizer that controlled the relationship of I/O components to the computer's central processing unit (CPU). The conservative giant and the adolescent science were sprinting into the future together.

Charting the Path of Input/Output

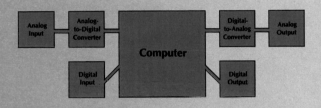

Even the most sophisticated stereophonic system is utterly useless if it lacks a way to pick up audio information from the recording surface. It is equally useless without sensitive speakers to translate that information into rich and resonant sound. A computer, too, for all its power, is nothing more than a clump of circuitry unless it has a way of taking data in, storing it for processing and then turning the processed results into actions or displays desired by the human operator.

Unlike stereo systems, which have just one job to do, computers are called upon to handle all manner of information about the world. Getting this information into the computer is the job of so-called input devices. These may be as general as computer keyboards or mice, or as specialized as sensors that can monitor air pressure in a wind tunnel or the temperature of a rocket engine. Often the information picked up by sensors must be translated into the ones and zeros of the computer's own language before the machine can work on it. This translation is performed by an analog-to-digital converter *(pages 22-23)*; without it all the power of the computer would go untapped. Data that has been processed by the computer can then be displayed on such output devices as video screens, printers or graphic plotters. It can also be used in other ways—guiding computer-controlled aircraft, for example, or rotating a bar of steel in a computerized manufacturing plant.

As illustrated in the drawing shown here, a computer's input/output, or I/O, process is made up of certain basic elements, whether the machine in question is a powerful supercomputer, a modest desktop model or the set of computers that help fly an experimental jet. Pages 28-31 trace the path data follows as it moves into and out of a computer system, and describe different methods for making the I/O process as efficient as possible.

Turning All Phenomena to Analog Signals

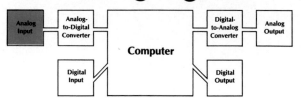

The information taken in at the beginning of the input process may be light, sound, heat, pressure or any number of other real-world phenomena. Each of these occurs as a continuum, with infinite gradations between extremes, and they require translation into another form before they are susceptible to the precise logic of a computer. Input devices called sensors initiate the translation process by converting the data into electrical signals of varying voltage.

Known as analog signals because they are in fact analogies of reality, the voltages represent fluctuations of the physical phenomenon that is being measured or observed. For example, a temperature sensor called a thermocouple produces a stronger voltage as temperature rises, a weaker one as it falls; a light-sensing photoelectric cell responds to light intensity in the same fashion.

But a varying analog signal is only a first step, for most modern computers employ a two-state, or binary, logic: Their circuits work only in on-off terms. Before analog input can complete its journey through the system, it must therefore undergo several additional changes.

An analog translation
In this metaphorical version of the genesis of an analog signal, a real-world phenomenon peels away from the earth like skin from a plump fruit, then passes through the portal of a figurative sensor. The sensor produces an analog electrical signal whose fluctuating peaks and valleys correspond precisely to the variations picked up by the sensor.

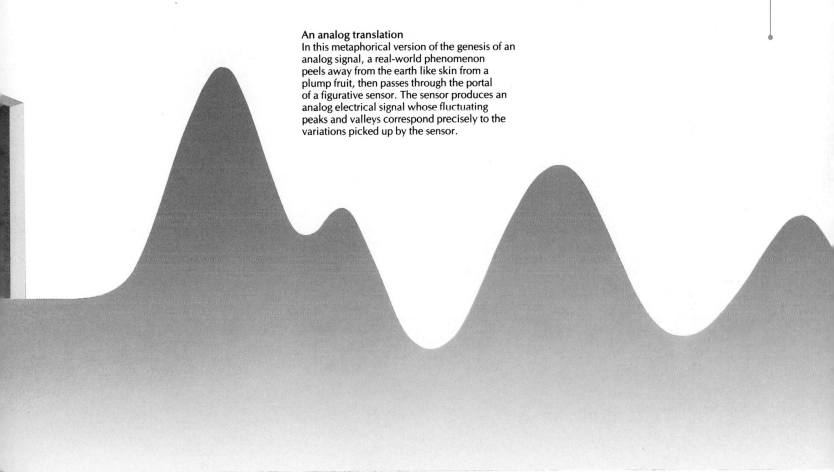

From Analog Signals to Digital Logic

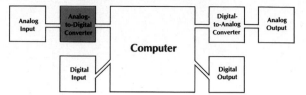

Before an electronic digital computer can interpret an analog signal for processing, the signal must be translated into the computer's binary language. This is accomplished by passing the signal through an analog-to-digital (A-to-D) converter, which transforms the varying voltages of the signal into a series of rapid on-off pulses. The pulses correspond both to the computer's yes-no, true-false logic and to the binary number system, which can express any number—no matter how large or small—as a combination of zeros and ones (box, right). In a digital computer, zeros and ones are represented by the off or on states of the tiny electronic circuits that make up the machine's central processing unit, or CPU, as well as its internal memory and other components.

To change an analog signal into a digital one, the A-to-D converter takes periodic readings, or samples, of the analog signal, translating the voltage at each sampled point into numerical values. Once the continuous analog signal has been thus reduced to discrete digital data, the information is ready to be fed into the computer for action.

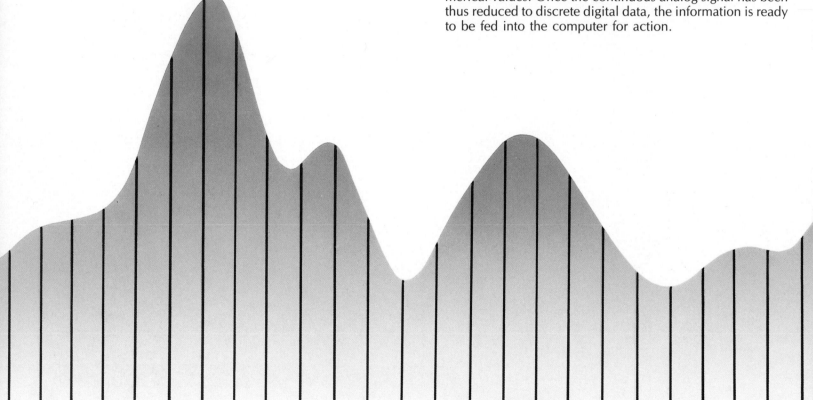

A digital translation
To change a continuous analog signal into a discrete digital one, an analog-to-digital converter samples the signal at regular intervals. These intervals must be very rapid—double the speed of the signal's highest frequency—to avoid a misleading conversion. At best, the digital signal can only approximate the analog original. As soon as the converter takes its lightning-fast readings, it assigns a number to each segment (right); the stronger the voltage the higher the number, the weaker the voltage the lower the number.

The Binary Beat

In the base-two binary number system, each place to the left of the one's place increases in value by a power of two. In the binary number 10110000, for example, ones mark places representing decimal values of 128, 32 and 16; adding those values produces decimal 176. A single binary digit is called a bit; eight bits are a byte. The largest decimal number that can be expressed in a byte is 255 (11111111). Computers handle information in units, or words, ranging from eight to 60 bits in length.

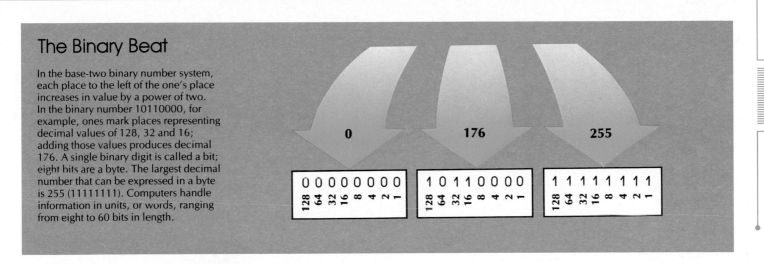

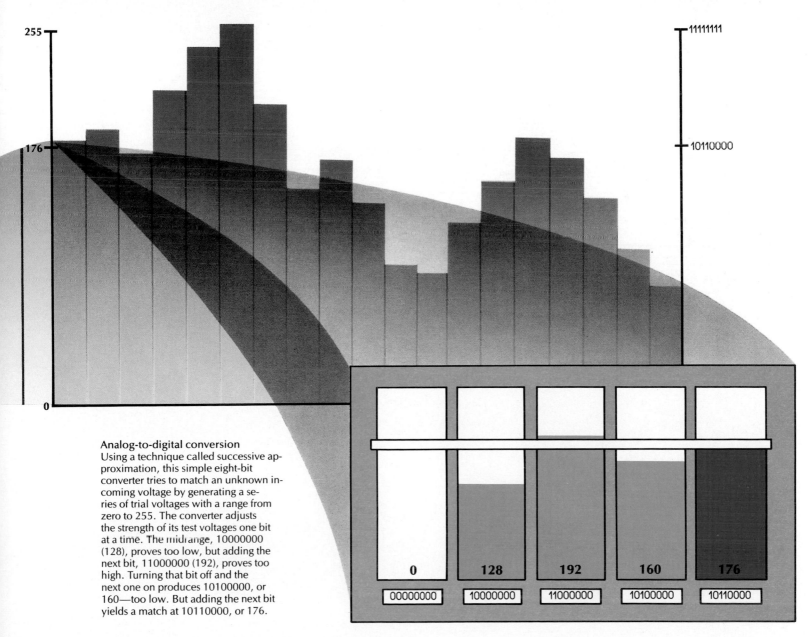

Analog-to-digital conversion
Using a technique called successive approximation, this simple eight-bit converter tries to match an unknown incoming voltage by generating a series of trial voltages with a range from zero to 255. The converter adjusts the strength of its test voltages one bit at a time. The midrange, 10000000 (128), proves too low, but adding the next bit, 11000000 (192), proves too high. Turning that bit off and the next one on produces 10100000, or 160—too low. But adding the next bit yields a match at 10110000, or 176.

Marching Orders for Bits and Bytes

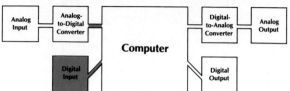

Once coded as binary pulses, information enters the computer in either serial or parallel fashion through electronic gateways called ports. A port is deemed either serial or parallel according to the arrangement of bits it is designed to handle.

In the serial mode, the bits that make up a computer word (the word length used here is eight bits, or a byte) stream one after another along a single path *(far left, top)*. At the port, they are lined up abreast to form units of whatever length the computer is designed to process. From that

Serial Port

1 0 1 1 0 0 0 0

1 0 1 1 1 0 0 0

1 0 1 0 1 0 0

Parallel Port

1 0 1 1 0 0 0 0

1 0 1 1 1 0 0 0

1 0 1 0 1 0 0 0

point on, the individual bits travel in parallel, as a unit.

Bits entering a parallel port arrive already abreast, having traveled on individual paths. This is much faster than serial transmission but has its own drawbacks. Beyond distances of 100 feet, synchronizing parallel signals is difficult and the cost of multiple wiring can become prohibitive. Thus, when signals must travel long distances—thousands of miles by telephone, for example—computer systems designers choose the slower serial method.

The Directness of Digital Input

Not all of the data entering a computer's input ports is analog in origin. Much of the information used by computers is digital to begin with, having been entered by means of such devices as keyboards, keypunch machines or magnetic tape. In this simplified digital input device, the binary equivalent of 176—10110000—has been keyed in with toggle switches representing a one (on) or a zero (off).

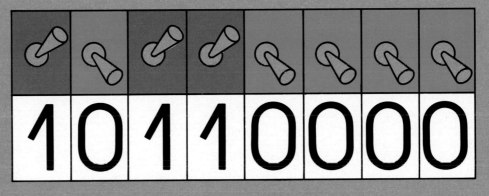

Road Map to the Inner System

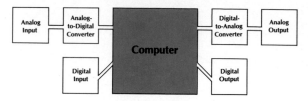

While some computers are more complex than others, certain components are common to all machines. The components may range in size from a single microchip to foot-square cubes of circuitry made up of many chips, but their functions remain the same.

The key element in every computer is the central processing unit (CPU), which serves as the machine's brain, the component that carries out instructions and directs the ebb and flow of data during processing. The CPU relies on information and instructions stored away in two types of computer memory: ROM, or read-only memory, and RAM, or random-access memory (RAM is also sometimes referred to as read-and-write memory). ROM's contents are permanent and remain intact even when the machine is turned off. The information in RAM can be changed at will—as when a new program is loaded into the machine from external storage—and is erased when power is shut off.

Other components common to all computers include clocks, which synchronize internal operations (and are sometimes built into the CPU chip itself); buses, the electronic circuits that link the computer's elements together; and the input/output ports. The stylized system pictured at right also includes two pieces of optional equipment—an input/output (I/O) controller and a direct-memory-access (DMA) controller—that are not found in every computer.

When external information comes into the computer through the input ports, it travels along the buses to the CPU, which stores the data in RAM. Later, the CPU may retrieve the data for processing according to directions stored in memory. The results can then be retained in memory or sent through an output port to a peripheral, there to be stored or translated into action of some kind. Pages 28-31 explore in detail the three major ways that computers control input and output: polling, interrupts and DMA.

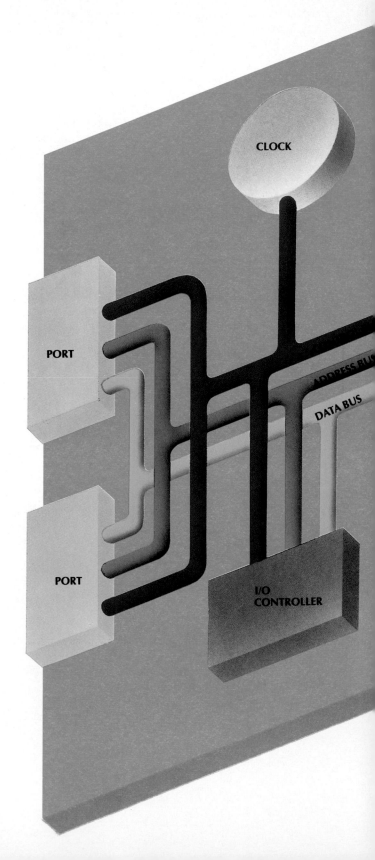

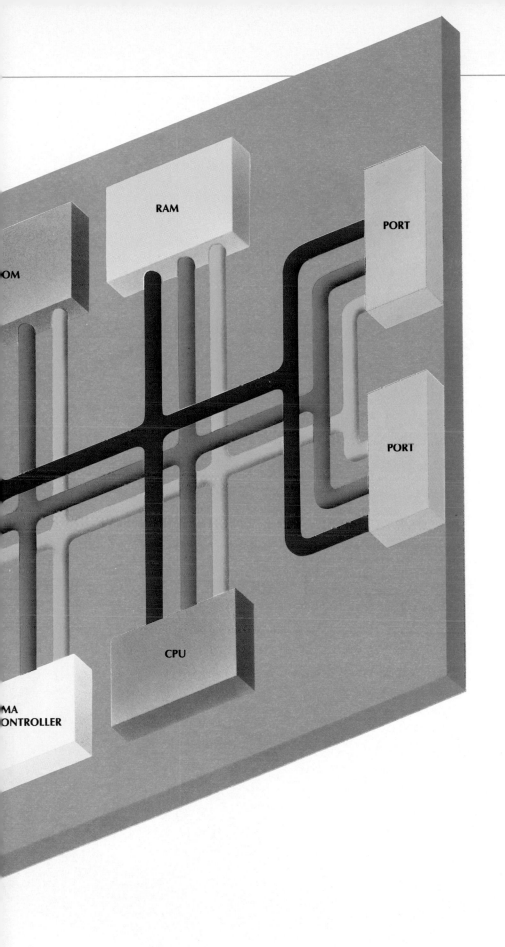

RAM

PORT

OM

PORT

CPU

MA
ONTROLLER

A Roster of Components

Ports mediate the flow of data into and out of the computer. They may be input, output or dual-purpose input/output ports, operating either in serial or in parallel.

Buses are internal pathways for information: Control signals travel on the control bus; data travels on the data bus to a destination whose address is carried on the address bus.

The clock pumps regular electronic pulses through the control bus, synchronizing all the activities of the computer.

ROM, the computer's permanent internal memory, holds essential information such as start-up instructions.

RAM is the temporary memory bank, the repository of programs and data that can be used or altered by the CPU.

The CPU serves as the brain of the whole computer system; it performs the machine's arithmetic and logical operations.

The I/O controller is usually found on large multiuser systems, where it handles routine input/output operations for the CPU.

The DMA controller, another piece of optional equipment, can bypass the CPU and provide for direct communication between peripherals and RAM.

27

Two Methods for the Regulation of I/O

With the entry of data into the computer, one of three fundamental techniques for controlling operations goes into action. The main steps in two of the most common input/output techniques, polling and interrupts, are shown conceptually at right and below.

In polling, the CPU must regularly check—or poll—each port in turn to determine if it has information for input or is ready to accept data for output. A port's status one way or the other is indicated by single-bit electronic signals, which are known as flags. Polling is simple but slow. It also wastes valuable CPU time, since the CPU must pause between executing processing instructions to conduct the poll of each port—just in case action is required. It is as if a host had no way of knowing whether or not a guest had arrived except by periodically going downstairs and opening the front door.

The interrupt technique requires more complex hardware and software but makes far more efficient use of the CPU's time and capacities. When this system is in play, the CPU concentrates on its essential business of processing data. When a port is ready for input or output, it transmits a signal—rather like the ringing of a doorbell—to the CPU, which only then takes a break from its processing and turns to the needs of the port in question. In this technique, predetermined priorities avoid confusion in case two or more interrupts are signaled simultaneously. The user also may choose to mask, or ignore, interrupts, with one exception: the power-failure interrupt. This nonmaskable interrupt, or NMI, tells the CPU it has only a few microseconds in which to store data before power failure shuts the system down.

Both polling and interrupts are used for input as well as for output, and neither method requires an I/O controller. For the sake of simplicity, the sequences here show only the input process; output is essentially the same process in reverse. The interrupt technique is shown with an I/O controller in order to demonstrate the function of that optional component.

Interrupts: Complex but More Efficient

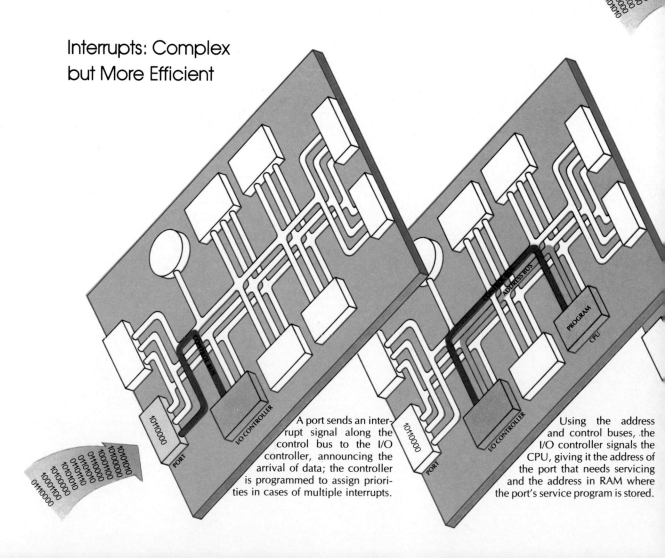

A port sends an interrupt signal along the control bus to the I/O controller, announcing the arrival of data; the controller is programmed to assign priorities in cases of multiple interrupts.

Using the address and control buses, the I/O controller signals the CPU, giving it the address of the port that needs servicing and the address in RAM where the port's service program is stored.

Polling: Simple but Slow

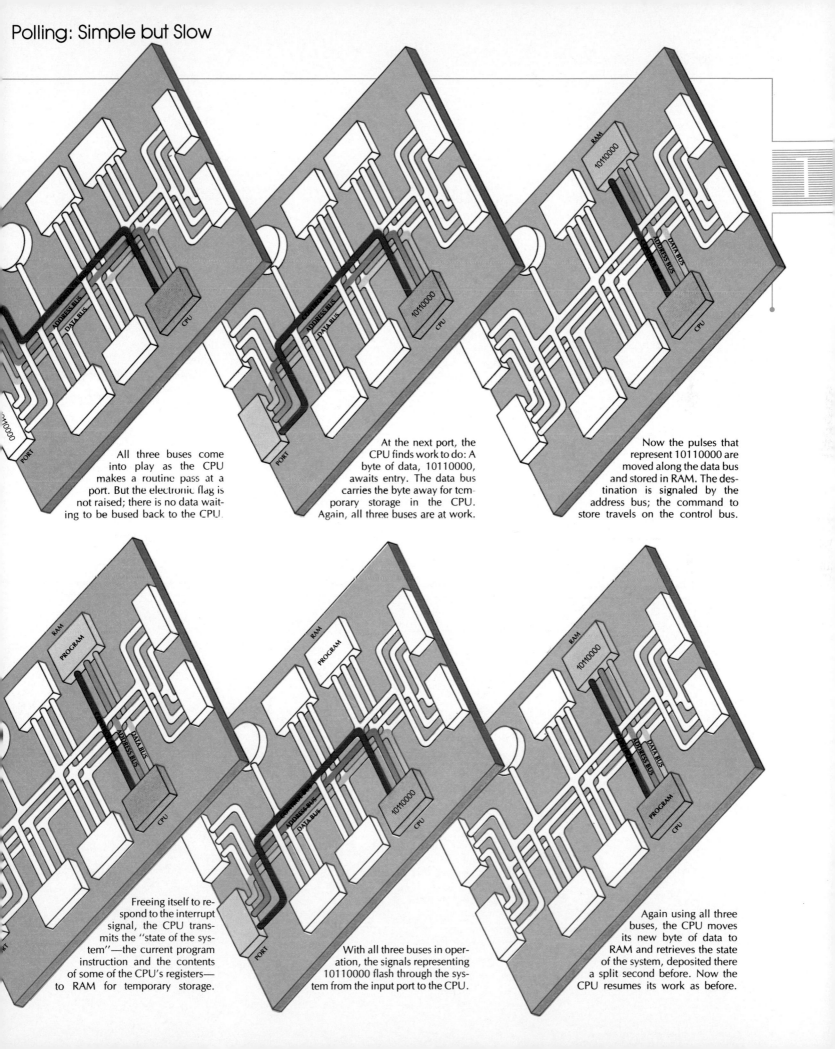

All three buses come into play as the CPU makes a routine pass at a port. But the electronic flag is not raised; there is no data waiting to be bused back to the CPU.

At the next port, the CPU finds work to do: A byte of data, 10110000, awaits entry. The data bus carries the byte away for temporary storage in the CPU. Again, all three buses are at work.

Now the pulses that represent 10110000 are moved along the data bus and stored in RAM. The destination is signaled by the address bus; the command to store travels on the control bus.

Freeing itself to respond to the interrupt signal, the CPU transmits the "state of the system"—the current program instruction and the contents of some of the CPU's registers— to RAM for temporary storage.

With all three buses in operation, the signals representing 10110000 flash through the system from the input port to the CPU.

Again using all three buses, the CPU moves its new byte of data to RAM and retrieves the state of the system, deposited there a split second before. Now the CPU resumes its work as before.

A More Direct Route to Memory

Many an urban highway system features a high-speed commuter lane that permits car poolers to whiz past congealed streams of rush-hour traffic. Direct memory access, or DMA, gives computer input and output a similar advantage, allowing data to zip directly into or out of memory without the relatively balky intervention of the CPU. In effect, the DMA controller steps in and takes over from the CPU as director of electronic traffic on the computer's network of buses.

There are several ways that the DMA controller assumes command of the bus system. In the most common version, the DMA controller receives an interrupt signal from a peripheral device and flashes a "hold," or suspend operations, message to the CPU. The CPU responds with a "hold-acknowledge" signal, relinquishes jurisdiction over the buses and then, in effect, takes a nap. Meanwhile, the DMA controller shunts data between RAM and the input or output devices.

The main advantage of using direct memory access is speed. Unlike the CPU, which is a generalist designed to perform many tasks, the DMA controller has just one job to do, and its circuits can be designed accordingly. DMA is thus employed with peripheral devices, such as the terminals used for colorful graphics displays, that are simply too fast for their input and output to be controlled effectively by the CPU. DMA is also useful in operations, such as loading data from modern fast disks, where input arrives in large bursts.

The sequence seen at top right illustrates the operations of the DMA controller in dealing with input. The bottom sequence shows how the DMA controller uses the same technique to handle output, sending data through a port for transmission to a peripheral device for storage, display or action.

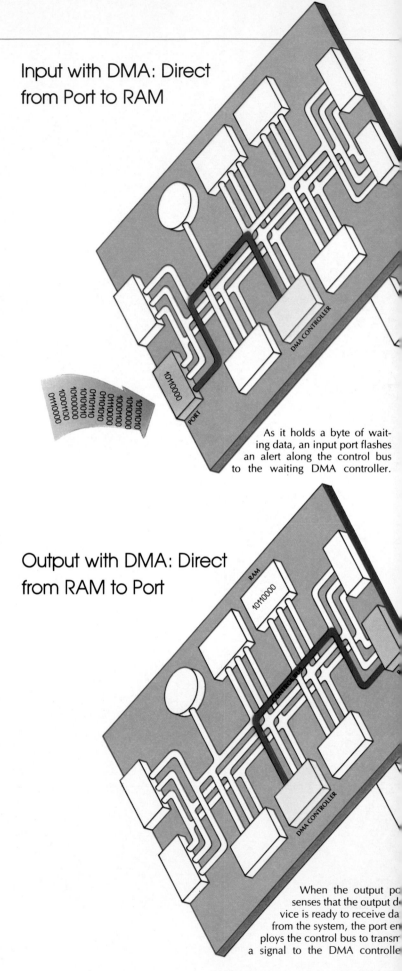

Input with DMA: Direct from Port to RAM

As it holds a byte of waiting data, an input port flashes an alert along the control bus to the waiting DMA controller.

Output with DMA: Direct from RAM to Port

When the output po senses that the output d vice is ready to receive da from the system, the port em ploys the control bus to transm a signal to the DMA controlle

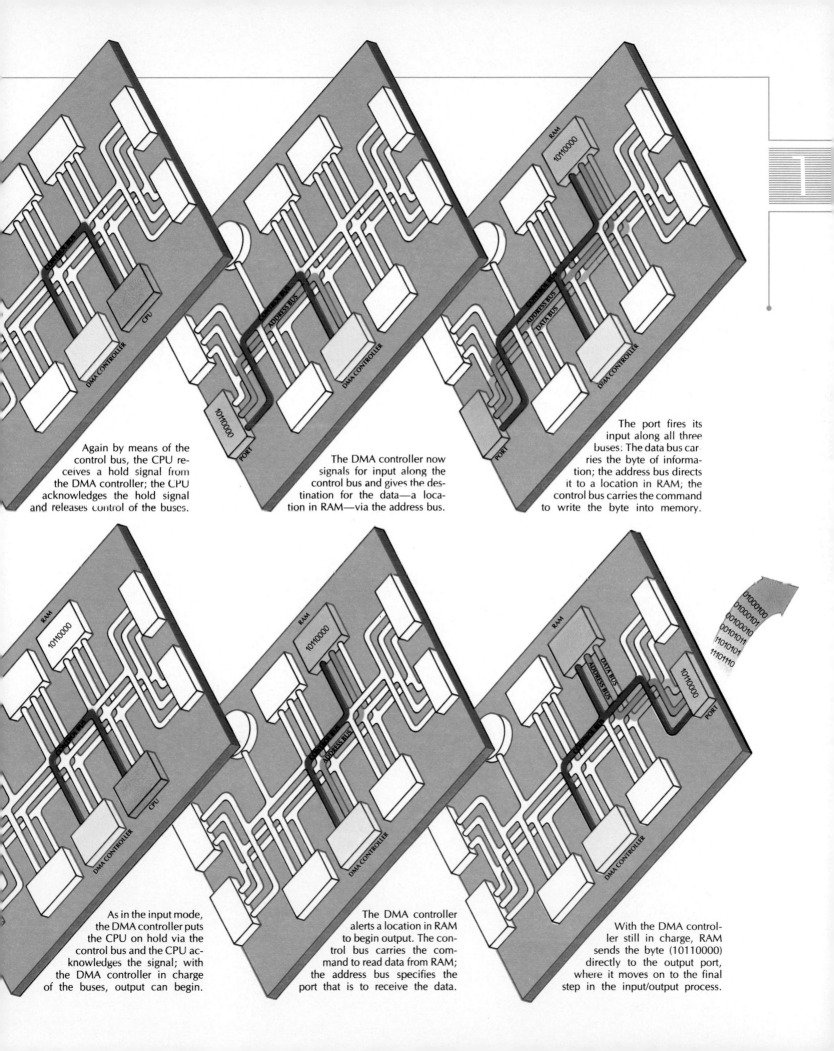

Again by means of the control bus, the CPU receives a hold signal from the DMA controller; the CPU acknowledges the hold signal and releases control of the buses.

The DMA controller now signals for input along the control bus and gives the destination for the data—a location in RAM—via the address bus.

The port fires its input along all three buses: The data bus carries the byte of information; the address bus directs it to a location in RAM; the control bus carries the command to write the byte into memory.

As in the input mode, the DMA controller puts the CPU on hold via the control bus and the CPU acknowledges the signal; with the DMA controller in charge of the buses, output can begin.

The DMA controller alerts a location in RAM to begin output. The control bus carries the command to read data from RAM; the address bus specifies the port that is to receive the data.

With the DMA controller still in charge, RAM sends the byte (10110000) directly to the output port, where it moves on to the final step in the input/output process.

Translating Data Back into Phenomena Again

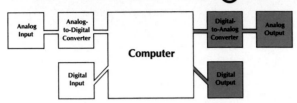

Like the incoming information that is fodder for the computer's central processing unit, output can take either analog or digital form, depending on the particular output device being used. Synthesizers that permit computers to deliver data as audible speech must translate digital output into analog signals that can activate a loudspeaker. In contrast, devices such as cathode-ray tubes, which display data as on a television screen, or printers, which produce results on paper, are designed to translate discrete units of digital output into corresponding discrete results on the screen or page.

Another digital output device is the plotter, shown here in stylized form. A plotter translates the binary signals sent by the computer into precise coordinates between which the pen travels to produce a graphic image.

Output, Analog Style

Analog output is made possible by a process exactly the reverse of the way analog input is changed to digital signals. As depicted at right, a converter turns on-off binary signals into a continuous analog signal. First, the converter assigns each byte or word of digital data a voltage keyed to the value of the binary number; this produces a jagged curve of abruptly fluctuating voltages. The curve is then passed through a special electronic filter and smoothed into a continuous analog signal. This signal in turn can drive an analog output device, such as a loudspeaker or the actuator that maneuvers a robot arm.

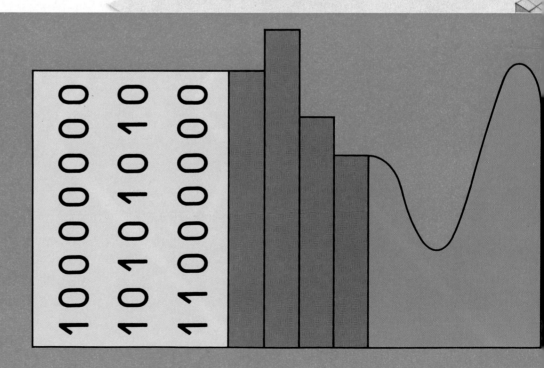

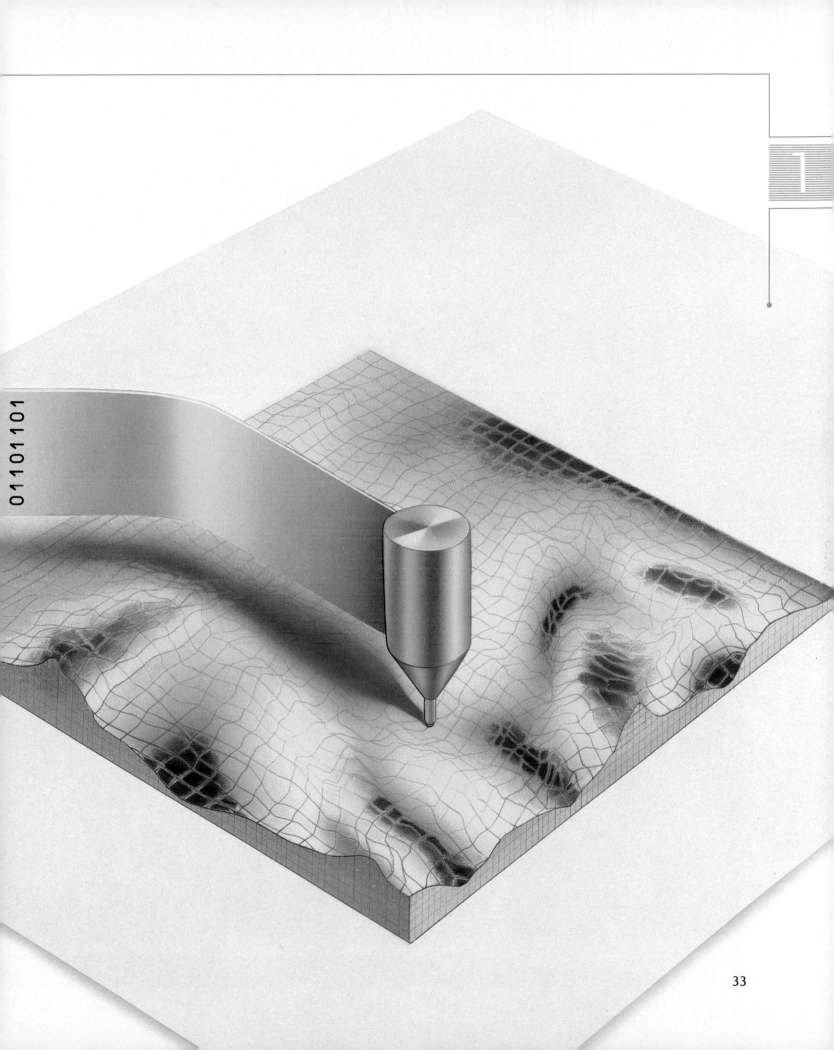

01101101

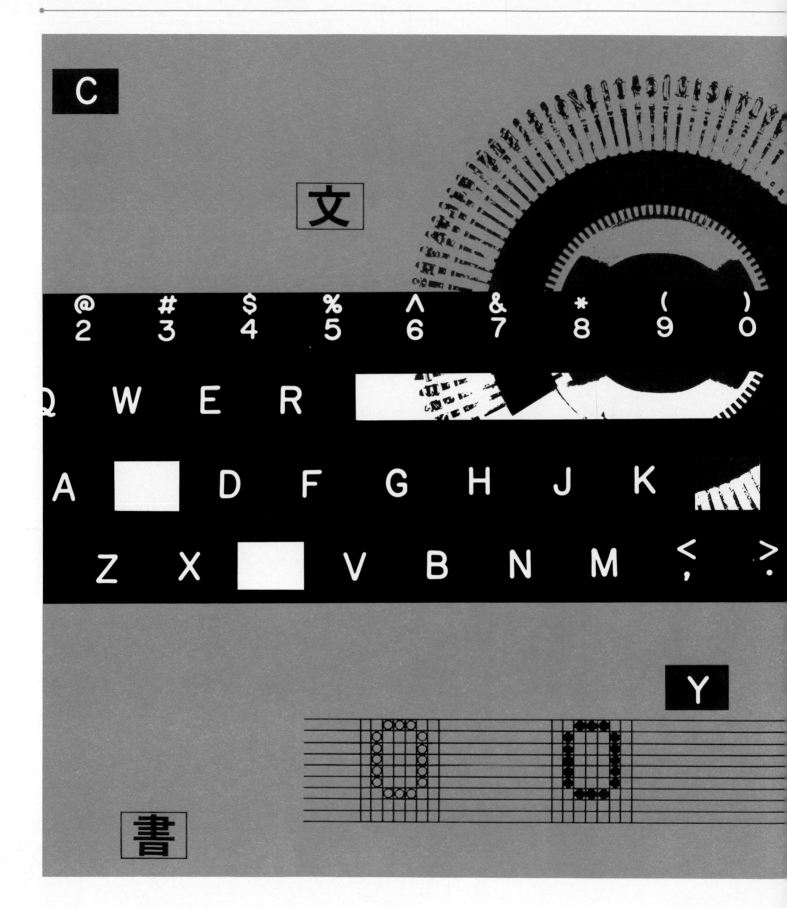

Evolving from Number Cruncher to Word Machine

Nothing so challenged the nimble-minded students who frequented the computer center at the Massachusetts Institute of Technology in the late 1950s as the quest for new ways to use the exotic machines they had access to. These young enthusiasts, among the first to call themselves hackers, were constantly experimenting with the school's TX-0 computer. And one day in 1959, an anonymous M.I.T. hacker made the happy discovery that he could use the computer's input/output equipment to produce letter-perfect term papers for the classes he attended when he was not immersed in hacking.

The TX-0 was an advanced machine, built with compact transistors instead of the bulky vacuum tubes that were then standard, and designed expressly for experimental applications rather than only for numerical computation. Its peripheral equipment included a Flexowriter, the typewriter-like machine used on SAGE and Whirlwind (page 13) to print characters as well as to punch coded holes in paper tape. In fact, Flexowriters had been intended originally to produce form letters that were the forerunners of today's familiar mass mailings, with their pseudopersonal salutations. Special codes punched in the tape automatically stopped the machine during the printing cycle so that the operator could key in different names, addresses and greetings on otherwise identical letters.

Initially, the students employed a Flexowriter to write computer programs and to print out the resulting data. Its great advantage as a producer of term papers was that hackers could use the stop-and-go capacity to punch corrections into the paper tape without the drudgery of having to retype entire pages. They then fed the corrected tape into a mechanical reader that interpreted the patterns of holes and instructed the Flexowriter to type out a manuscript, error free.

By the fall term of 1961, M.I.T. had received a powerful new computer, the PDP-1 (for Programmed Data Processor). This machine was the gift of the Digital

Typewriters have entered the computer age, and the result is a division of their labor into two parts: input, symbolized here by a keyboard, and output, represented by a dot-matrix form and a daisy wheel from a computer printer. These functions, amplified by the power of the computer, have yielded one of high technology's most useful applications—word processing.

Equipment Corporation, headed by M.I.T. alumnus Kenneth Olsen. Where the tape-reading device on a Flexowriter was entirely mechanical and could read only 10 characters per second, the reader on the PDP-1 was equipped with light-sensitive photoelectric cells and ran at 400 characters per second. Such a boon did not go unexploited for long.

Stephen Piner, one of M.I.T.'s most ingenious student hackers, soon wrote a program for the PDP-1 designed to help him and his comrades edit software for the computer—and, not incidentally, also edit their term papers—at high speed. Piner christened his program Expensive Typewriter, an acknowledgment of the irony of harnessing such a sophisticated machine for a text function usually done with an ordinary typewriter.

Access to the PDP-1 was so precious that Piner and his friends continued to punch out the first drafts of their manuscripts on a separate Flexowriter. "We could justify in our minds using the computer to make corrections to existing text or programs," recalled one of Piner's colleagues, Alan Kotok. "But it was considered impolite and bad form to use the computer to originate text."

EASING THE WORD BURDEN
Though the hackers at M.I.T. only vaguely sensed it, they were blazing a path into the future. Piner's Expensive Typewriter was one of the first word-processing programs ever written; many others would follow. Today, more people employ the computer as a versatile (but not so expensive) typewriter than for any other purpose. Users of every stripe sit at computer keyboards, flick their fingers and watch words appear on the monitor as if by magic. Secretaries turn out perfectly typed letters every time, authors write and revise their novels and—yes—a new generation of students compose term papers with a minimum of drudgery.

Although the enlistment of computers in producing text is relatively recent, attempts to mechanically ease the labor of writing go back nearly three centuries. In 1714, Britain's Queen Anne granted a patent to an engineer named Henry Mill for having invented "an artificial machine or method for the impressing or transcribing of letters singly or progressively one after another, as in writing." Unfortunately, theory proved easier than practice. Mill did not manage to build a workable writing machine; nor did dozens of other inventors who pursued the same vision. No one succeeded until the 1860s, when a Wisconsin newspaper editor and printer named Christopher Latham Sholes tackled the problem.

There was in Sholes a touch of the modern-day hacker. He left newspaper work when he received a political appointment as customs collector for the Port of Milwaukee, but he remembered the tedious hours he had spent writing articles and editorials with a quill or a steel-nibbed pen: There had to be a better way, and he was determined to find it. Since Sholes's new job was relatively undemanding—Milwaukee being less than a major international seaport—he found plenty of time to indulge his passion for tinkering. In a local machine shop, Sholes and an associate, Carlos Glidden, developed an apparatus for numbering book pages consecutively. From this simple machine evolved the first practical typewriter.

Sholes patented the device in 1867. Six years later the Sholes and Glidden machine was put on the market by E. Remington and Sons, the respected firearms firm that would become Remington Rand and in 1951 would market UNIVAC, the first commercial computer in the United States. After the Civil War, Reming-

Introduced in 1873, the pioneering Sholes & Glidden typewriter combined handsome design with less than convenient operation. The machine had hanging type bars that struck the roller from underneath, making it impossible for the operator to read what was typed without raising the carriage assembly.

ton had diversified from weapons making into the manufacture of sewing machines. The first typewriters reflected the change: They were decorated with gay floral designs and were mounted on sewing-machine stands rigged so that stepping on the treadle automatically returned the carriage.

The first model of the Type-Writer, as Sholes named the device, had distinct limitations. For the high price of $125, the customer got a machine that typed only in capital letters. Because the key-activated type bars were hidden beneath the carriage, the operator had to lift the carriage to see what had been typed.

The Type-Writer was not an immediate success, but it earned high praise from some of its early purchasers. One was a former typesetter named Samuel Clemens, who wrote books under the pseudonym Mark Twain. Using the hunt-and-peck method (the touch system was not developed until several years later), Twain wrote a letter to his brother:

I AM TRYING T TO GET THE HANG OF THIS NEW F FANGLED WRITING MACHINE, BUT AM NOT MAKING A SHINING SUCCESS OF IT. HOWEVER THIS IS THE FIRST ATTEMPT I EVER HAVE MADE, & YET I PERCEIVETHAT I SHALL SOON & EASILY ACQUIRE A FINE FACILITY IN ITS USE...I BELIEVE IT WILL PRINT FASTER THAN I CAN WRITE. IT PILES AN AWFUL STACK OF WORDS ON ONE PAGE. IT DONT MUSS THINGS OR SCATTER INK BLOTS AROUND.

A few years later, Twain became the first author to submit a typewritten manuscript to a publisher. (According to Twain, the book was *Tom Sawyer*, though scholars have identified it as *Life on the Mississippi*.) Twain in fact became so enthusiastic about mechanical aids to writing and printing that he later invested $300,000 in a typesetting machine. It proved impractical, and he went bankrupt.

Other companies soon introduced their own versions of the typewriter, including so-called visible machines, which enabled the operator to see what was being typed, and models with a shift key to allow for both upper- and lower-case letters. The efficiency of these improved machines—as well as the fact that they did not "muss things or scatter ink blots around"—ultimately overcame the doubts of businessmen, and the typewriter entered the workplace.

One notable holdout against the new technology was the growing mail-order firm of Sears, Roebuck. Sears worried that typewritten letters were too impersonal, and even after the typewriter became widely accepted in the 1890s, Sears insisted that its secretaries write all correspondence by hand so as not to offend the company's farmer clientele with the newfangled "machine-made" letters.

The typewriter not only revolutionized office procedures but also changed the way that offices were staffed. By providing socially acceptable employment for women outside the home, it became a powerful instrument for their emancipation, opening up what in most companies had been an all-male domain. The writing machine, observed Christopher Sholes before his death in 1890, "is obviously a blessing to mankind, and especially to womankind. I builded wiser than I knew."

Soon enough, however, women began to realize that they had been liberated from the kitchen stove only to be enslaved by the typewriter. It was an unforgiving machine, infuriatingly faithful to the pressure of the fingers on the keys: One mistake and the whole page had to be retyped. The development of the electric typewriter during the 1920s did nothing to solve the problem. The electric was faster and easier on the fingers, but unintended pressure on the wrong keys could send several type bars flying in error.

When the first computers came into being during World War II, it was only natural that modified typewriters be employed to print output from the central processing units. Within a decade, they were being used to prepare input data as well. The problems of error and tedious revision remained, however—and seemed even more frustrating considering the high speed of the CPUs.

THE SEARCH FOR A SOFTWARE SOLUTION

Pioneers in the emergent field of computers looked for solutions in software rather than hardware. Weary of having to code every instruction in the two-state yes-no, zero-one logic of the computer's binary language, they began seeking simpler ways to communicate with their machines. Their first efforts resulted in new codes peppered with letters and short words taken from the English language. Maurice Wilkes, then at Cambridge University, is credited with being the first to create one of these so-called assembly languages. In 1949, he devised one for use in EDSAC, the first operational computer that could store its programs in internal memory. At the same time, researchers at M.I.T. were developing a more advanced language for their unfinished Whirlwind.

Typically, an assembly language consisted of commands couched in easy-to-remember symbols. The letters *SU,* for example, might tell the computer to subtract; *TS* might instruct it to transfer to storage the data that followed. Each symbol replaced a long sequence of ones and zeros in the program. The symbols were automatically converted back into binary code, which was all the computer understood, by a program known as an assembler.

Conversing with the machine in the rudiments of human language instead of ones and zeros was the first step toward the development of higher-level programming languages—and a major advance toward using the computer to manipulate text. Further progress came in 1955 at M.I.T.'s Lincoln Laboratory with the completion of the TX-0, the machine that would serve M.I.T.'s innovative student hackers a few years later. The TX-0 was a programmer's delight. In addition to having a 65,536-character memory—large for its time—it was equipped with the most up-to-date devices for input and output. The TX-0 had a display oscilloscope and a photosensitive tool called a light pen for altering the display. Moreover, its Flexowriter had been modified so that it was on-line—rigged to permit direct keyboard input without first punching out the cumbersome paper tape.

The TX-0 was waiting when Jack Gilmore, a young aeronautical research engineer, returned to M.I.T. after flying carrier planes for the U.S. Navy during the Korean War. As a graduate student in 1951, Gilmore had written the first assembly program for Whirlwind. Now his colleagues showed him the TX-0 and said, "Find out what you can do with this thing."

Gilmore responded first by writing a series of utility programs. They were intended, he said, "to help us with our dirty work" by enabling researchers to modify and debug (eliminate errors in) their programs on-line. As a method of communication between programmer and computer, Gilmore's creation was a forerunner of today's operating systems, the group of programs that perform such duties as keeping track of where data is stored in temporary memory or on disks or tape. One program, called FIND, enabled the user to search another program for specific words or instructions. The operator also could initiate a high-speed print-out of data in a program simply by typing in the code word PRINCE.

Gilmore's utility system could even ask questions, providing a foretaste of the give-and-take between user and machine now called interactive computing. For example, in a routine for punching out a corrected paper tape for storage—which Gilmore had labeled PUNCHY—the computer asked, "DO YOU WANT A TITLE?" If the programmer typed in "YES," PUNCHY then asked, "WHAT IS THE TITLE?" and the user could type in some identifying word.

Gilmore's next project took him deeper into the computer manipulation of text. In the hope of designing an improved input device for the TX-2, an improved version of the TX-0 (there was no TX-1), he wrote an experimental program in 1957 that he called the Scope Writer because it enabled him to generate typewriter-like characters on the computer's oscilloscope with a light pen. The eight-by-eight-inch screen had 512 dots across and 512 down. "We would fill the screen with dots," Gilmore later recalled, "and then, using a light pen, we would shut off the ones we didn't want, essentially drawing the character."

A KEYBOARD ON THE SCREEN

Gilmore and his co-workers created a so-called program editor to manipulate these characters. It enabled the computer to display on the bottom half of the oscilloscope a simulated keyboard that contained 200 keys—roughly three times the number on the old Flexowriter. Each key was represented by a dot on the screen. Touching a dot with the light pen would cause the appropriate character—the letter a or the number 8, for instance—to appear on the top half of the screen, which simulated a printed page. There were even provisions for superscripts, as in 80° F., and subscripts, as in H_2O.

Perhaps the most interesting aspect of the program editor was its simulation of so-called function keys, which presaged today's computer keyboard. Touching one dot, for example, would return the typewriter's carriage; other dot-keys provided for such functions as tabular indent and vertical and horizontal spacing.

The program editor also allowed for the swift editing and revision of what the light pen had already "typed" on the simulated page. Operators could mark their position in the text by means of an indicator, or cursor, that could be moved around the screen for making insertions. The user could also employ the light pen to delete characters and, with a later modification of the program, move words and entire paragraphs around the scope.

Some of the advances in Gilmore's experimental Scope Writer program were incorporated two years later into an input mechanism developed for the TX-2. The new device, called the Lincoln Writer, was a kind of super Flexowriter, with an expanded keyboard that included Greek letters, mathematical symbols, and such functions as subscripts and superscripts. It also had provisions for simultaneous communication with the computer and its paper-tape punch.

Without quite realizing it, Gilmore and his colleagues had created the essence of high-speed word processing, which Stephen Piner would carry a step further with his Expensive Typewriter program. Still, that was not their goal. The researchers at M.I.T., as at most other computer laboratories, were engaged in data

A Hard Habit to Break

QWERTY: Purposely Slow

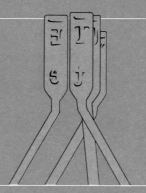

The familiar QWERTY keyboard *(below)*, named for its first row of letters, was actually designed to slow typists down. Its 19th-century inventor, Christopher Sholes, originally laid out the keys of his Type-Writer in alphabetical order. He soon found that the primitive wooden type bars *(right)*, which were slow to fall back into place, jammed as the hunt-and-peck typists of the day became more proficient. So Sholes scrambled the keyboard, moving the most commonly typed letters to positions less speedily accessible to a typist's index fingers. Adopted by later generations of touch-typists, this purposely inefficient layout has remained virtually unchanged to the present day.

The most commonly typed letters—
E, T, A, O, N and *I*—are scattered
on the QWERTY keyboard.

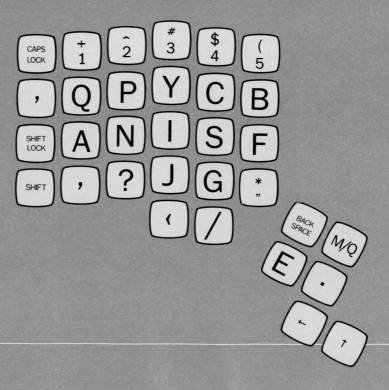

40

Keyboards have evolved from wire and wood to plastic and silicon, but their QWERTY key arrangement has not changed in 100 years. Outdated and inefficient, yet dear to the hearts of trained typists all over the world, the QWERTY keyboard *(below, left)* is still the standard, although speedier and more comfortable alternatives have been around for decades.

One such alternative is the Dvorak Simplified Keyboard *(below),* first demonstrated by its inventor, August Dvorak, in 1932. A University of Washington professor of statistics, Dvorak placed the letters that occur most often in English on the home row, where a typist's fingers come to rest. Using keys from this row alone, a typist can produce about 3,000 common English words; using the home row in QWERTY produces only about 100.

An even greater departure from the QWERTY layout is the P.C.D.-Maltron design *(bottom),* an electronic keyboard in-troduced in the late 1970s by the British team of Lillian Malt and Stephen Hobday. On a split keyboard contoured to fit each hand, keys rise to different heights to accommodate the natural disparity in finger lengths. The Maltron also places the most common symbols under the strongest fingers.

Proponents of both the Dvorak and Maltron keyboards offer as evidence remarkable improvements in typing efficiency. Speed increases of up to 50 percent over the QWERTY keyboard are claimed for the Dvorak, while professional typists who have switched to the Maltron have been able to type as fast as 200 words per minute, versus a typical rate of 60 words per minute on the QWERTY layout. Despite their promise of higher performance, neither the Dvorak nor the Maltron has yet succeeded in supplanting the QWERTY keyboard. Modern electronic keyboards may be easy to reprogram, but QWERTY-trained typists apparently are not.

The Dvorak keyboard places the most commonly used letters on the home row.

On the split Maltron keyboard, the most commonly used keys are placed under the strongest fingers: the space key under the right thumb, the *E* under the left thumb. A typist may switch to the QWERTY lay-out simply by pressing the *M/Q* key.

processing, which meant crunching numbers. Their primary motive in creating Scope Writer and Lincoln Writer was not to manipulate text for its own sake but, as Gilmore wrote in a 1959 memo, "to improve the language through which information is exchanged between man and machine."

In this they had certainly succeeded. And even as software advances continued, the practical application of text manipulation received a push from an innovation in hardware.

The new breakthrough involved the familiar combination of computer technology and that old stand-by, the typewriter. But this time the impetus came from the corporate world rather than the academic. IBM, which had emerged as a dominant force in computer data processing, had gone into the electric-typewriter business years earlier, buying out a small manufacturer called Electromatic during the Depression. IBM engineers had even designed a paper-punch I/O system that, in other hands, yielded the Flexowriter.

THE ADVENT OF THE STATIONARY CARRIAGE
In 1961, IBM introduced the Selectric, a machine that not only radically reshaped the electric typewriter but became an essential component in a new system of text manipulation. The thing most obviously different about the Selectric was its printing mechanism. On a single print element shaped like a golf ball, it combined all of the type characters and symbols that traditionally had been inscribed on separate type bars. Moreover, this spherical element moved rapidly across the page while the rest of the typewriter remained stationary. In nearly all previous typewriters, the carriage did the moving. (One notable exception was the first crude electric typewriter, a printing-wheel machine, patented in 1872 by Thomas A. Edison, that evolved into the modern ticker-tape printer.)

The Selectric set a new standard for office typewriters and soon became a versatile workstation for computers as well. As an input device, it benefited from the simple combination of codes by which each keystroke tilted and rotated the print element. As an output device, it offered two important features—a maximum printing speed of 15 characters per second, 50 percent faster than type-bar typewriters, and the stationary carriage, which enabled continuous-feed paper to move more easily through the typewriter.

Even before its commercial introduction, the Selectric had demonstrated its value as a printer on IBM's advanced Model 7030 computer, popularly known as "Stretch." Stretch was developed during the late 1950s to perform computations for the Atomic Energy Commission and to manipulate letters and other code symbols for the top-secret cipher systems of the National Security Agency. The machine, which was then the fastest in the world, got its name from IBM's attempt to stretch the state of the art in computing.

Although Stretch had been designed for highly classified government work, the computer became available for inspection by visitors to the IBM lab in Poughkeepsie, New York, a few months before the Selectric was officially introduced. To preserve the secrecy of the new golf-ball typing element, security-conscious IBM employees covered the open slot at the top of Stretch's typewriter with a plain piece of cardboard. A few visitors peeked beneath the cardboard, but evidently none of them comprehended the novelty of what they saw.

Stretch turned out to be a commercial failure that cost the company $20 million. Its Selectric component, however, was an overwhelming success as a typewriter. And in 1964, three years after the typewriter appeared, IBM engineers integrated the Selectric's print element into a system that signaled the biggest improvement in mechanized text manipulation since Sholes's invention: They mated the Selectric with magnetic tape for storing data. The tape was essentially an electronic version of the old Flexowriter paper-punch tape; instead of perforations, the presence or absence of a magnetic spot on oxide-coated plastic tape represented the binary digits one or zero. A combination of seven of these bits of electronic information encoded a particular character.

Output from the Selectric keyboard went simultaneously to a sheet of paper in the typewriter and to the magnetic-storage device. Whenever an error was made, the typist simply backspaced and typed the correct character over it. Though the strikeover showed up on the paper, only the correction appeared on the magnetic tape because the act of backspacing electronically erased the error.

Magnetic storage thus provided a laborsaving backstop for the typist, who could type rapidly without worrying about mistakes, which could easily be corrected. The corrected text could then be printed out on the Selectric or stored on the magnetic tape. IBM later upgraded the system by substituting magnetic cards for the tape. Cards were easier to handle and file than tape, and each card held 5,000 characters—a little more than one full page of single-spaced typing.

IBM at first referred to working on its souped-up Selectric as "power-typing." But in 1965, an IBM employee in Germany named Ulrich Steinhilpher coined a term that better described the electronic manipulation of words: *Textverabetung*. This translated into English as "word processing," and the name stuck.

Selectric dominated the marketplace for IBM into the early 1970s. But by then, computer technology was advancing at explosive speed. As hardware became smaller and less expensive because of mass production of the tiny integrated circuits that now constituted a computer's innards, full-blown word-processing systems began to appear in rapid-fire succession. The companies that made them, unlike IBM, tended to be lilliputian in size and new to the office-equipment business. In 1971, the Lexitron Corporation introduced the first commercial word-processing system equipped with a CRT screen. In 1972, the Vydec Corporation went two steps beyond, offering the first system complete with CRT screen, electronic printers, and a floppy-disk device for magnetically storing programs and data. The specially coated plastic disk, which in fact had been invented by IBM to serve the company's mainframe computers, provided greater capacity and faster access time than either magnetic cards or tape.

TAKING ON THE GIANT
But the most effective challenge to IBM's obsolescent Selectric system was mounted by An Wang, a Chinese-born physicist who had come to the United States in 1945 to earn a Ph.D. at Harvard and later became an American citizen. In 1951, Wang founded his own company, Wang Laboratories, in a single room above an electrical-fixtures store in Boston. There, he engineered one-of-a-kind electronic products to fill specific customer needs.

In 1972, Wang entered the word-processing market with a system that used magnetic-tape cassettes and the IBM Selectric for input and output. "At one time we were the largest single buyers of IBM typewriters," a former Wang employee

A Word-Processing Challenge

文書の作

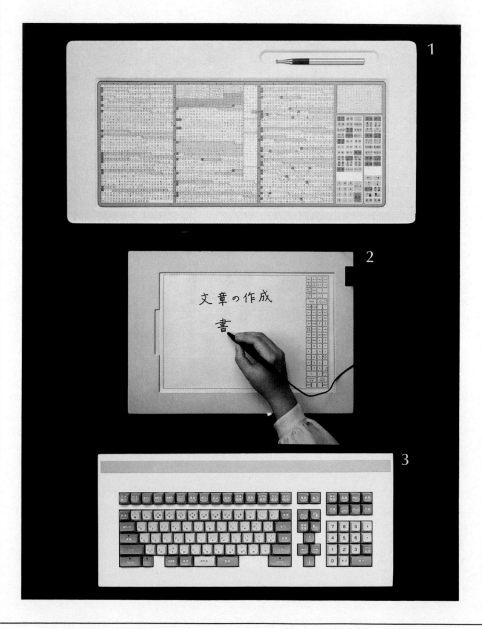

1

2

3

文 書 の 作 成

A

文 □ の 作 成 文 書 の 作 成

B

文 書 の 作 sei 星 製 政 性 成 文 書 の 作 成

C

成

Written Japanese is a daunting mix of three sorts of characters: Chinese-derived ideographs called *kanji*, of which more than 3,000 are in common use; dozens of shorthand-like phonetic characters called *kana;* and the 26 letters of the Roman alphabet, known as *romaji*. Persons skilled in the use of a Japanese typewriter are so rare that, until recently, nearly all correspondence in Japan was conducted painstakingly by hand. Now systems such as the three shown at left enable the characters to be produced by computer.

One system centers on a touch-sensitive pad *(1)* that displays 3,327 *kanji* characters as well as the *kana* and *romaji* alphabets; using a stylus to select each character is thus a slow process unless the keyboard has been memorized. A second system, featuring a digitizing tablet *(2)*, is faster; it relays the shape of a hand-drawn character to the computer, which compares it with characters stored in memory. If the computer cannot recognize a shape, it leaves a flashing rectangle *(B, top line)*, substituting the correct character after the user rewrites it *(second line)*.

The phonetic-conversion method *(3)* is preferred by most Japanese typists. After entering syllables in *kana* or *romaji* *(C, top line)*, the typist presses a key that tells the computer to find the correct transliteration in a special table in memory. Often, as in this example, a *romaji* syllable could be represented by many *kanji* homophones, which sound alike but have different meanings. The computer presents likely *kanji* alternatives *(second line)*, and the typist selects the appropriate one. The *romaji* syllable disappears, replaced by the chosen *kanji* character *(third line)*, to complete the phrase shown above: *"bunsho no sakusei,"* or "writing a document."

recalled. "We would rip out the most wear-intensive parts, replace them and throw the old ones in the town dump."

Within five years, the Wang WPS, or Word-Processing System, featured multiple workstations and programs that were easily modified for processing words in foreign languages as well as in English. The WPS offered a CRT screen for reading text and controls for avoiding accidental deletions; anyone who knew how to type could learn to use the system with little training. By 1980, the one-room company had become a giant itself, controlling more than one third of the world market in word processing—surpassing even IBM in this field.

The introduction of the microcomputer broadened the word-processing universe to embrace the home as well as the office. Proliferating software such as Electric Pencil, Screenwriter and the best-selling WordStar made it possible to transform even the least expensive home computer into a word processor.

Professional authors were among the most enthusiastic adherents to this new way of writing. As early as 1973, novelist John Hersey experimented with writing fiction on a Yale University computer and became an instant convert. Others followed; although some serious writers resisted the idea of creating their art on a machine, the computer's speed and reduction of tedium overcame the recalcitrance of most. By the early 1980s, popular programs not only processed an author's words but checked them for correct spelling as well. Writers working at home could even avoid the trip to the post office by hooking up their word processors to devices called modems and transmitting their prose—computer-coded in electronic impulses—to the publisher over the telephone.

No matter which of the world's many languages authors may write in, their words must be translated, letter by letter, into the computer's universal language, the binary code. For English, with only 26 letters in its alphabet, this process is relatively uncomplicated. The American Standard Code for Information Interchange (ASCII), developed in 1961, assigns to each character seven binary digits. (An eighth digit, positioned at the beginning of the sequence, is either ignored or used as a check on the accuracy of transmission. The eight digits, or bits, constitute one byte.) Mathematically, there are 128 different ways in which seven ones and zeros can be combined. Thus the ASCII system allows for 128 different characters, more than enough to encode the upper- and lower-case Roman alphabet, decimal numerals and various other symbols used in English and most other Western languages.

By contrast, calligraphic languages such as Chinese and Japanese are exceedingly difficult to encode. Accommodating their thousands of ideographic characters requires complex strings of binary code in which two or more bytes must be assigned to each character. One result of this is that Japan has lagged in the development of software for processing its own language, even though it is a leader in the production of computers. Some of the best word-processing programs for Japanese, in fact, have been created in the United States.

A PLETHORA OF PRINTERS
In the years following the introduction of the Selectric, a number of other hardware innovations appeared. One important breakthrough was the daisy-wheel printer. It was announced in 1970 by Diablo Systems, a company founded by former employees of the Singer Corporation's Friden division, manufacturer of

the old Flexowriter. In the daisy-wheel mechanism, characters on the ends of petal-like spokes radiating from a rotating flat disk are struck by a hammer and imprinted on paper through an inked ribbon. More than twice as fast as the Selectric, the daisy wheel soon replaced the familiar golf-ball print element for high-quality work.

Even as the daisy wheel flourished, an even faster desktop printer was introduced in 1971 by another new company, Centronics. This device, called the impact dot matrix, printed patterns of dots in the shape of an alphabetic character or a numeral. IBM had been working with the principle of using dots to form characters since the early 1950s. The concept was made commercially viable, however, by the invention of the microprocessor, the so-called computer on a chip. The microprocessor stores information received from the computer and directs the firing of an array of tiny pins contained in a print head. Each pin pushes individually against the inked ribbon to imprint a single dot on the paper. Combinations of these dots form the desired character—in italics or boldface if the printer is so instructed. Unlike machines with solid-font daisy wheels, dot-matrix machines can also print complex graphic images such as photographs and drawings (page 58).

As automated mass production caused the price of microprocessors to plummet in the late 1970s, Japanese-made dot-matrix printers came to dominate the microcomputer market. By the mid-1980s, some 40 percent of all the printers sold in the United States were products of Epson Corporation, a part of Seiko-Epson, a huge conglomerate based in Japan. Epson got both its name and its foothold in computer printers by a roundabout route. In 1964, Seiko set out to design a new timing device for the Olympic Games, for which Japan was the host country. The resulting device, which fathered the immensely popular quartz wrist watch, contained a mechanism for printing out a record of a runner's time. The printer was a great success at the games and was later adapted for use in desktop calculators and cash registers. It was marketed as the EP-101 (EP for "electric printer"). From those beginnings evolved the company that now produces nearly 12 million printers a year. Seiko named its new division Epson because the dot-matrix printer was the "son" of the EP-101.

LASER-BEAM PRECISION
Conventional dot-matrix machines can achieve speeds of up to 600 characters per second, but only at a sacrifice of crispness; the dots making up each character are too few to render the fully formed look of a character made by a high-quality typewriter. This limitation does not apply, however, to a newer and faster dot-matrix printing system: the laser printer. IBM introduced the first commercial laser printer in 1975. Instead of using a print head with its array of pins, the printer employs a microprocessor-controlled laser beam and technology borrowed from simple photocopying to turn out as many as 215 pages per minute (page 59). The device imprints some eight million microscopic dots upon a single page—more than enough to ensure book-quality printing.

The laser printer represents one more step in the fulfillment of the earliest hackers' aspiration: to expand the boundaries of the computer's potential by communicating easily with the machine in words and getting impressive results in that same human language.

Team Players for Instant Interaction

Perhaps the most salient characteristic of modern computing is the nearly instantaneous interaction possible between the system and its human operator. In most systems, the interaction takes place through the medium of a keyboard and screen (generally called a monitor), with results given permanent form by a printer. Over the years, these progeny of long-ago marriages—between computers and typewriters, and between computers and televisions—have undergone constant refinement. As illustrated on the following pages, keyboards, screens and printers have become sophisticated instruments for getting information into and out of a digital computer.

Keyboards and screens may attach to the computer as individual input and output devices, or the two may be linked to form a terminal, which may then be connected to the computer as a single I/O device. (Terminals are common in multiuser systems, which can permit hundreds of individuals to share the same central computer.) In either configuration, the keyboard acts as the control panel through which the operator enters data and commands. The monitor displays this input and the computer's response.

Computer keyboards differ from conventional typewriters in several ways. For one thing, a computer keyboard has a number of additional keys that perform special communicating functions. Also, keyboards are equipped with their own microprocessors, which coordinate the digital signals passing to and from the computer. The signals have no intrinsic meaning except whatever is assigned by system designers or programmers. The same keyboard may thus type English one moment and Greek the next.

Finally, the typing and printing elements of a computer system are independent of each other; in a typewriter they are inextricably linked. Press a key on a computer keyboard, and the result appears on the screen rather than on paper in the printer; a special command is usually needed to initiate printing. This independence is one source of a computer system's power and flexibility. For example, an operator can type a form letter, store it for a period and later print out multiple copies at speeds far greater than human typists could hope to achieve.

Secrets of a Computer Keyboard

A computer keyboard looks like the front half of a typewriter: It consists of a panel of keys marked with letters, numbers, commands and other symbols. But there the resemblance ends. Typewriter keys are simply triggers. They set in motion mechanisms that type characters on a page. Computer keys have a much more generalized role: They initiate electronic signals that record the location and order of keystrokes; those signals will later be assigned any of a wide variety of meanings, and the immediate result may even be invisible to the typist.

Although keyboards employing typewriter-like keys are the most common kind, many keyboards are equipped with membrane key panels—touch-sensitive switches underneath a plastic surface. Membrane key panels are frequently used to control computers in applications with a limited variety of input. In factories or restaurants, for example, the keys may be labeled with commands, such as START or STOP, or with symbols that represent items for sale, such as ice cream or french fries. Because membrane key panels are too sensitive to serve for accurate touch-typing, they are not suitable for tasks that require the entry of large amounts of data.

Underneath a computer keyboard is a grid of wires. Each key is poised above an intersection of wires, ready to close an electrical contact when the key is pressed. Because any keystroke will affect both a horizontal row and a vertical column of the grid, the keyboard's microprocessor needs only to monitor the rows, which are fewer in number than the columns. The microprocessor does this by using electrical current to scan each row in sequence, thousands of times a second (left). The scan goes on whether the keyboard is in use or not.

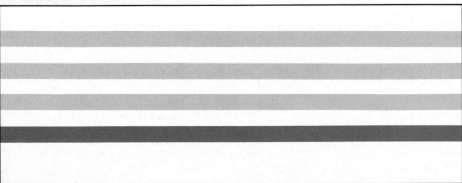

After perhaps thousands or millions of negative results from its row scanning, the microprocessor detects a row containing a closed circuit. To find out which of the score of keys located on that particular row is the active one, the microprocessor begins scanning by columns for the first time, after quickly recording which row triggered the column scan.

Because only one key can activate a given row and column simultaneously, the pressed key's identity is revealed as soon as the column scan detects an active column. The microprocessor records and transmits the key's identity as a "key code." As it scans for fresh key presses, the microprocessor ignores the already identified key until the operator's finger releases it, allowing further keystrokes to be located while the first key is still depressed.

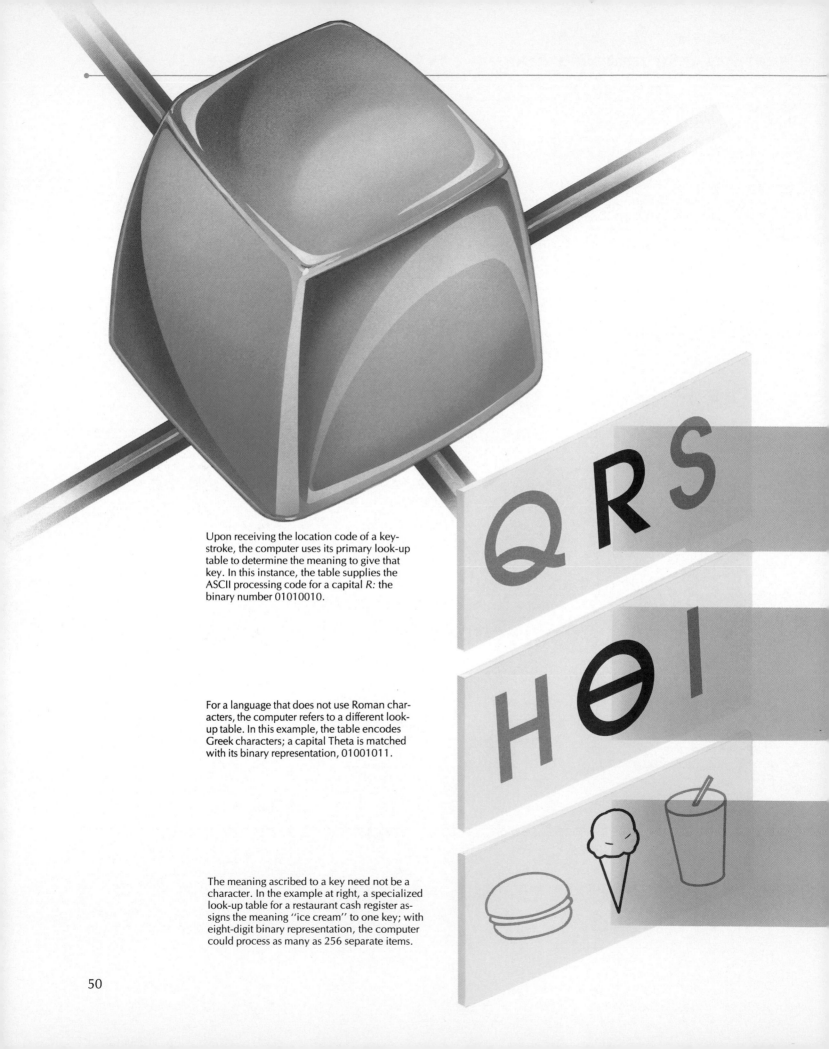

Upon receiving the location code of a keystroke, the computer uses its primary look-up table to determine the meaning to give that key. In this instance, the table supplies the ASCII processing code for a capital *R:* the binary number 01010010.

For a language that does not use Roman characters, the computer refers to a different look-up table. In this example, the table encodes Greek characters; a capital Theta is matched with its binary representation, 01001011.

The meaning ascribed to a key need not be a character. In the example at right, a specialized look-up table for a restaurant cash register assigns the meaning "ice cream" to one key; with eight-digit binary representation, the computer could process as many as 256 separate items.

Matching Codes to Their Meanings

The signal a keyboard microprocessor generates has no meaning other than as a code describing the location of a key that has been pressed. Before the computer can process a signal, it must translate that code into meaningful information. An electronic list called a look-up table correlates each key-location code with a binary number that is an expression of a meaningful symbol—a letter or a numeral, for example; the computer employs this binary number during processing.

A look-up table can be located in the permanent memory of a computer or in its keyboard; ordinarily, it defines keys according to most computers' usual functions: the entry of numerical data, for example, or word processing in a particular alphabet. Some programs may require a different look-up table that assigns new meanings to the keys for specialized applications. Thus a computer that normally processes keystrokes as Roman letters and numbers can interpret the same keystrokes to mean items for sale or mathematical symbols.

Computers for office-related applications in Western countries usually convert key codes into ASCII (American Standard Code for Information Interchange), a standard that uses 128 binary numbers to represent upper- and lower-case letters, Arabic numerals, typographical symbols and a variety of codes that instruct the computer to perform such functions as backspacing and sounding its bell or beeper. A set of standard codes for other alphabets has been established by the International Standards Organization (ISO).

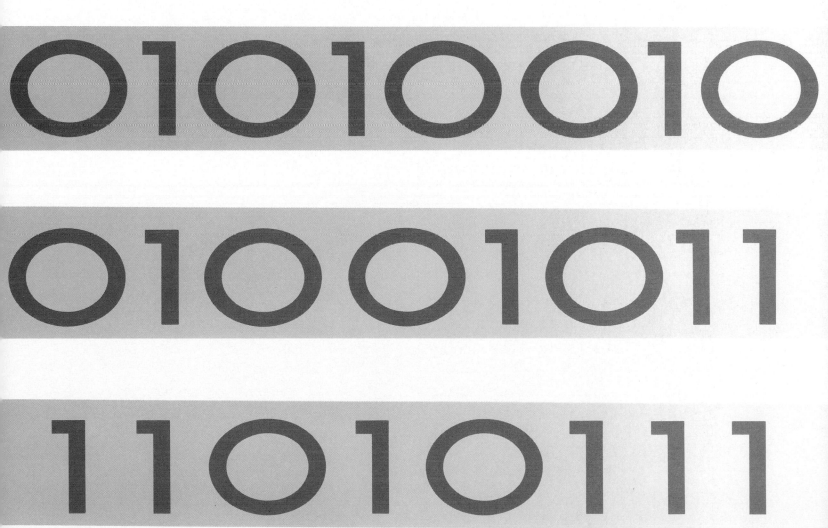

The Electronic Pointillist

A computer displays its output as shapes—whether letters, numbers or pictures—on a screen or a printer. Typically, the shapes are formed with dots of light or ink encoded by binary numbers. In most computers, text and graphics are handled somewhat differently.

Text output is generally mediated by a special chip called a character generator. This chip receives character codes intended for output and translates them, one at a time, into uniform-size blocks of zeros and ones (below). Each zero or one controls a single dot of the displayed image (on a screen,

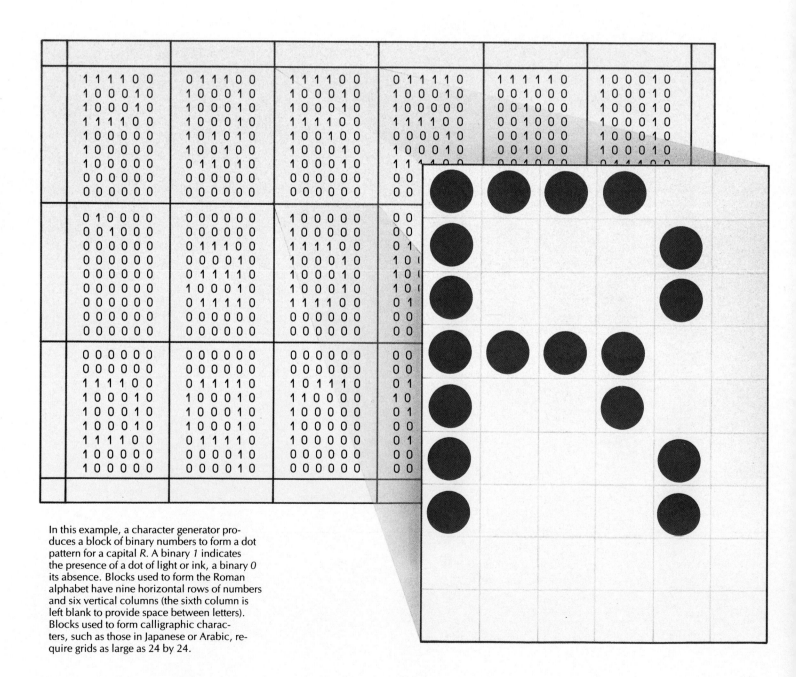

In this example, a character generator produces a block of binary numbers to form a dot pattern for a capital R. A binary 1 indicates the presence of a dot of light or ink, a binary 0 its absence. Blocks used to form the Roman alphabet have nine horizontal rows of numbers and six vertical columns (the sixth column is left blank to provide space between letters). Blocks used to form calligraphic characters, such as those in Japanese or Arabic, require grids as large as 24 by 24.

the many thousand such individually lighted points are called pixels, or picture elements). Together, the zeros and ones of a block are a map of that character—a map that already exists in the character generator's memory and hence reduces the demands on the computer's central processor and main memory: Since each character's shape is encoded in 54 binary digits, the computer achieves a large gain in efficiency by storing those shape instructions in the character generator and then calling them up with a shorter code (such as the eight-digit ASCII) each time the character is needed.

Similar block templates are sometimes used to produce relatively small graphic shapes—rocket ships in a video game, for instance. But most graphic images are treated as one-of-a-kind creations: The computer does not tap a preexisting archive of digital data. The computer also works with the whole image—rather than a small portion—in the point-by-point process of composition.

Graphic output, such as the picture of the cherries above, is also made up of tiny dots. In this example, the picture is created by superimposing four separate patterns of dots *(right),* one for each of the colors—magenta, cyan, yellow and black—used to make a printed image. In a video image, the intensity of each color on a screen—red, green and blue—may be varied to produce a much wider range of colors.

Creating an Image on a Video Screen

In most computers, the display screen is a cathode-ray tube (CRT), a device based on the same technology as that employed in television sets *(below, left)*. CRT screens—often called monitors—have been refined over the years to improve such attributes as contrast and color. Perhaps the greatest advances have been in resolution, which governs the screen's ability to produce fine detail. Specialized CRTs used in film making can display as many as nine million pixels

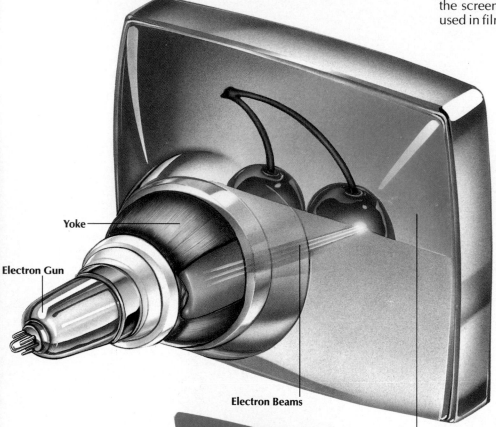

Yoke

Electron Gun

Electron Beams

Phosphor Layer

In a CRT, an electron gun in the narrow neck of the tube projects a beam of electrons toward the broad screen at the front, which is coated on the inside with phosphors that glow briefly when struck by the electrons. En route to the screen, the beam passes through an electromagnetic yoke that deflects it according to changes in the yoke's vertical and horizontal magnetic fields. The computer controls these variations and thus the patterns the beam traces on the phosphors. In a color CRT, three separate beams are generated, each exciting a different color in the pixels.

A raster-scan CRT forms images by casting electron beams in a horizontal pattern on the screen, moving from left to right, top to bottom. In a monochrome monitor, a single electron beam is switched rapidly on and off, so that only a portion of the screen pixels are illuminated while others are left dark to form the contrasting areas of the image. In a color monitor, the three beams that excite red, green or blue phosphors in the pixels are also switched on or off, and the varying intensities of the three basic colors can create as many as 16 million hues.

A vector CRT outlines images with a continuous beam rather than with the on-off pulse of a raster-scan device. The electron beam of a vector CRT is guided by the yoke directly from one point of the image to the next and can move diagonally as well as horizontally and vertically. The sharp, so-called wire-frame images that result are best suited for applications such as engineering. However, the method is relatively slow and cannot easily produce realistic solid images.

per screen, as opposed to 64,000 in a television-like home-computer monitor. The result is a picture as sharp as a photograph in a magazine.

The demand for portability has led to the development of flat-panel displays *(below)*. Smaller and lighter than CRTs, these screens are also less fragile, depending on a compact, solid design rather than on the careful alignment of delicate components inside a glass vacuum tube.

Flat-panel displays are grids with thousands of tiny electronic elements, arranged in columns and rows, that either darken or emit light when a current is applied to them. Images are formed by translating the computer's binary output into on-off instructions for each intersection of the array. There are three main types of flat-panel displays: In liquid-crystal displays, liquid crystals at intersections appear to darken when turned on; in gas-plasma and electroluminescent displays, the intersections glow to produce the image.

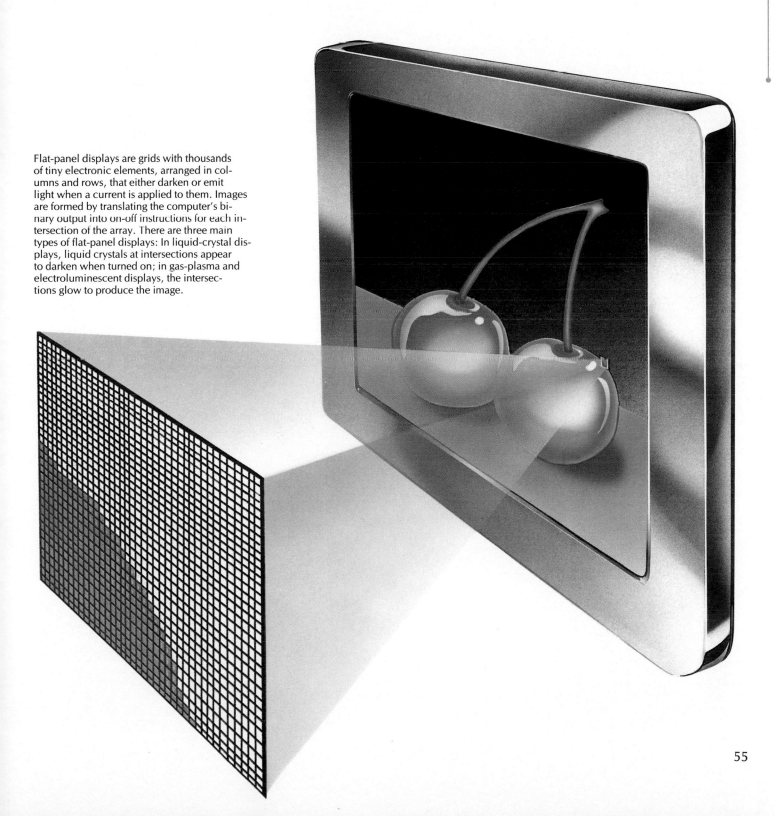

Printers That Make an Impact

Printers—output devices that make a permanent paper copy of a computer's work—fall into two broad categories: impact printers, which operate by pressing an inked ribbon against paper, and nonimpact printers. The choice is usually governed by the relative importance of quality, speed and cost.

Impact printers either make fully formed characters *(below, left)* or create characters from patterns of dots *(below, right).* The first kind generally produces a sharper result. The second, called a dot-matrix printer, is usually more economical, and it can be programmed to produce a variety of type faces or to print graphic images. Printers of fully formed characters range in speed from those that print characters one at a time, at rates as low as 10 characters per second, to those that print an entire line at once, generating thousands of lines per minute. Dot-matrix printers range from low-priced models that commonly deliver about 100 characters per second to expensive, high-volume machines that print 600 lines per minute.

Some nonimpact printers *(page 58)* also employ the dot-matrix technique, while others use technology similar to that of office copiers. The latter offer the flexibility of dot-matrix printers combined with a print quality approaching that of single-character impact printers.

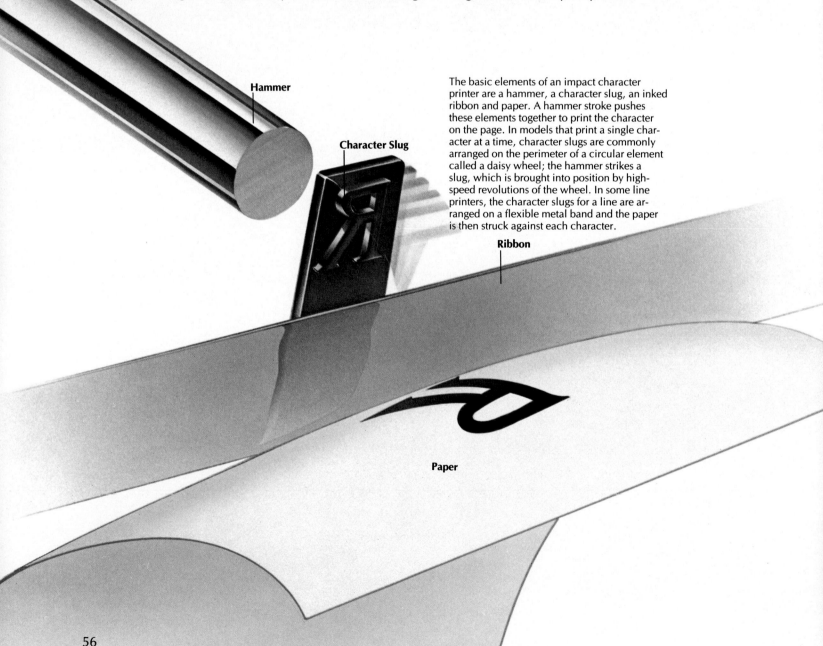

Hammer

Character Slug

Ribbon

Paper

The basic elements of an impact character printer are a hammer, a character slug, an inked ribbon and paper. A hammer stroke pushes these elements together to print the character on the page. In models that print a single character at a time, character slugs are commonly arranged on the perimeter of a circular element called a daisy wheel; the hammer strikes a slug, which is brought into position by high-speed revolutions of the wheel. In some line printers, the character slugs for a line are arranged on a flexible metal band and the paper is then struck against each character.

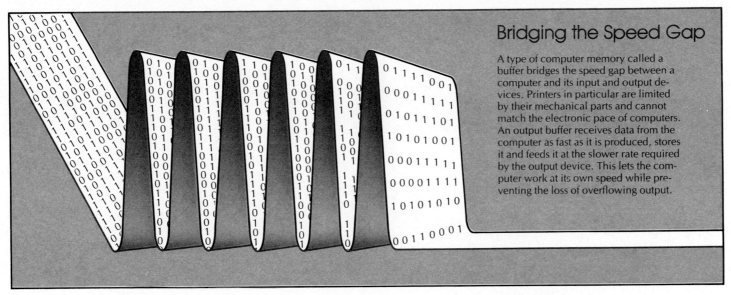

Bridging the Speed Gap

A type of computer memory called a buffer bridges the speed gap between a computer and its input and output devices. Printers in particular are limited by their mechanical parts and cannot match the electronic pace of computers. An output buffer receives data from the computer as fast as it is produced, stores it and feeds it at the slower rate required by the output device. This lets the computer work at its own speed while preventing the loss of overflowing output.

The print head of an impact dot-matrix printer consists of a set of pins arranged in one or more vertical columns. Each pin acts as an independent hammer, leaving a dot when it presses the ribbon against the paper. As the print head moves horizontally across the paper, the pins are fired hundreds of times in different combinations to create the dot patterns of individual characters. In this example, a nine-pin head has just completed the five columns of dots used to form an upper-case *R*.

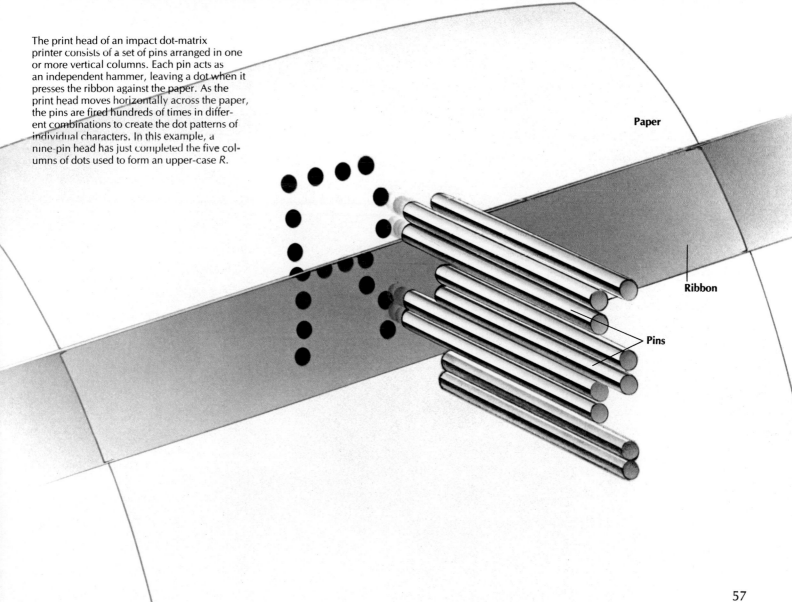

Paper

Ribbon

Pins

Producing an Image the Nonimpact way

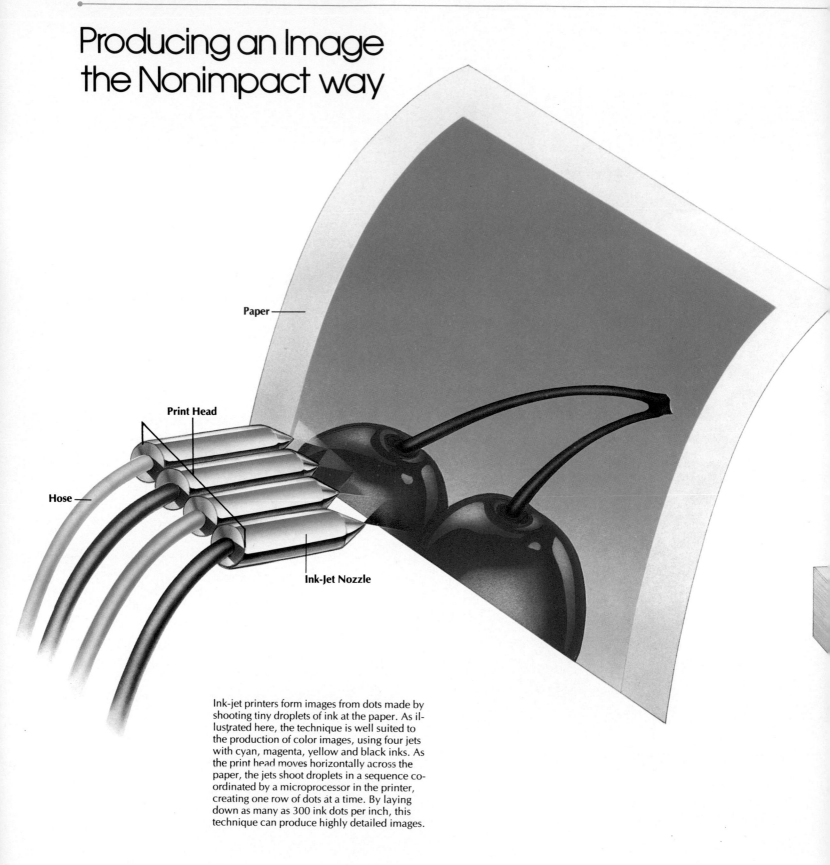

Paper

Print Head

Hose

Ink-Jet Nozzle

Ink-jet printers form images from dots made by shooting tiny droplets of ink at the paper. As illustrated here, the technique is well suited to the production of color images, using four jets with cyan, magenta, yellow and black inks. As the print head moves horizontally across the paper, the jets shoot droplets in a sequence coordinated by a microprocessor in the printer, creating one row of dots at a time. By laying down as many as 300 ink dots per inch, this technique can produce highly detailed images.

Electrophotographic, or laser, printers produce an entire page at a time. A small laser (1), turned on and off millions of times each second by a microprocessor, bounces a light stream off a hexagonal mirror (2). The reflected light neutralizes portions of the surface of a positively charged print drum (3), creating a latent reverse image. The drum is then dusted with a positively charged fine powder, or toner (4), which sticks only to the neutral areas (5). When the negatively charged paper (6) contacts the drum, the toner is attracted to it, forming the desired image (7). The image is fused to the paper by a combination of heat and pressure (8). As the finished page is produced (9), the drum is cleared of its electrical charge, cleaned and recharged for the next cycle.

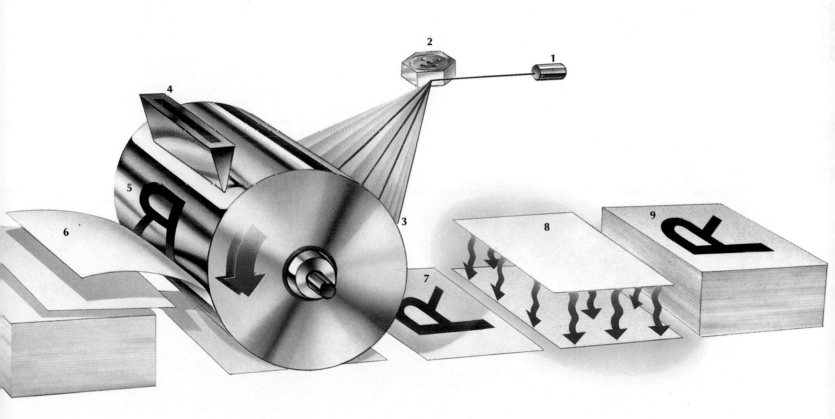

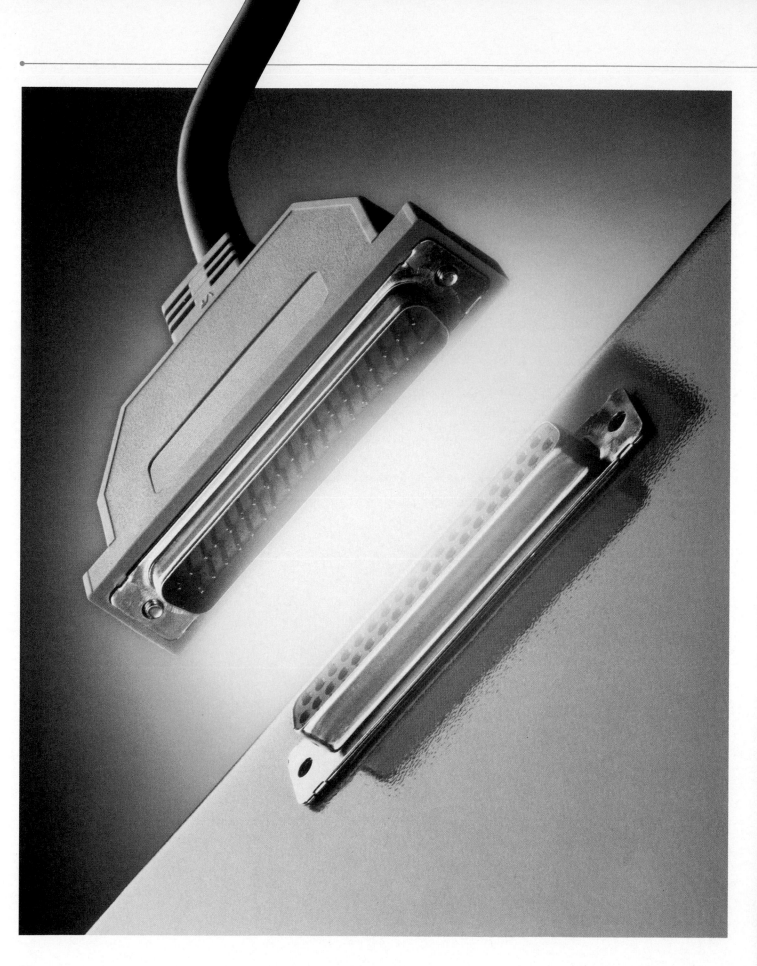

En Route to Compatible Computing

On April 7, 1964, International Business Machines—the colossus of the computer industry—held 77 press conferences in 15 countries to make what IBM chairman Thomas Watson Jr. called "the most important product announcement in company history." Given the corporation's stature in the computer field and its known aversion to hyperbole, these words were riveting. And events proved that they were absolutely justified.

As it happened, IBM announced not just one machine that day but a whole family of them. System/360, as the line of products was called, debuted with six models of varying size and price. According to one estimate, the research, development and manufacturing effort required to launch six machines simultaneously cost the company five billion dollars, more than twice what the United States had spent on the *Manhattan Project* during World War II to develop the atomic bomb.

With the benefit of hindsight, IBM's decision to invest in System/360 seems almost inevitable. At the time, however, it was a risky move that faced stiff internal opposition and was greeted with head-shaking skepticism by competitors. In essence, IBM was doing nothing less than gambling the corporate equivalent of its life, its fortune and its sacred honor on a project whose design would make the rest of the company's computers obsolete. System/360 was a daring departure from the technological status quo—so much so that it promised to change the whole computer industry's approach to input and output.

The executive perhaps most responsible for IBM's gamble was T. Vincent Learson, who, since joining the company in 1935, had worked exclusively at bringing new products to market. In 1959, Learson—an imposing man six feet six inches tall—had been made vice president in charge of the company's two major engineering centers, the General Products Division, in Endicott, New York, and the Data Systems Division, in Poughkeepsie. Neither center had an especially dazzling reputation for boldness or originality. Although IBM was the undisputed leader in the computer field at the time, it drew its success more from salesmanship and customer service than from exceptional engineering. This was a matter of increasing concern to Learson, Watson and other high-level executives.

For a variety of reasons, including internal rivalries that were resulting in a proliferation of competing IBM machines, Watson and Learson decided late in 1961 to map out an overall engineering strategy. Their instrument was a committee staffed by representatives of all major company divisions and dubbed SPREAD, for systems programming, research, engineering and development. In effect, Watson and Learson locked the 13 committee members in a room—

The symbolic mating of a plug *(top)* with a computer port illustrates a crucial breakthrough in computer development: the advent of so-called compatible machines. Introduced by IBM in 1964, standardized components made possible the explosive growth that followed in the production and use of I/O equipment.

actually a motel near Greenwich, Connecticut—and told them not to come out until they had established guidelines for the next generation of IBM machines. Chaired by Bob O. Evans, head of planning and development for the Data Systems Division, the committee worked for 60 exhausting days.

The often-heated discussions swirled around two untried concepts that were deemed desirable for IBM's future computers. The first was that any new machines should be capable of handling the full range of computing needs, from the logical and computational powers required by the scientific community to the data-processing powers needed in business (the name "360" represented this 360-degree capability). Before the early 1960s, computers were designed for either scientific or business applications. But as the decade began, more and more customers were trying to run business applications on scientific machines and vice versa, a practice that had not gone unnoticed by IBM.

MACHINES THAT WORK TOGETHER

The second concept was that the new computers should be compatible with one another. At the time, IBM had 15 or 20 different engineering groups turning out machines with only limited ability to share programs or exchange data. This incompatibility was in fact common throughout the industry; each model of computer possessed both a unique central processing unit, or CPU, and a unique I/O interface, the physical and electronic specifications for connecting devices such as keyboards and printers. Programs written according to the internal instructions of one CPU could not run on another CPU; peripherals engineered to work with a specific type of I/O interface could not be connected to any other machine.

From a marketing standpoint, incompatibility was a double-edged sword. Since buying a different brand of computer would mean scrapping an expensive collection of both software and peripherals, IBM customers were unlikely to send their business elsewhere. But by the same token, a customer who might want to upgrade from a small IBM computer to a larger one would face similar disincentives.

Not everyone at the Greenwich meeting believed that a line of compatible machines was possible, nor was anyone very sanguine about building dual-purpose computers. IBM's managers feared that, by creating machines for both scientific and business applications, they would end up with hybrids that could do neither job very well. As Evans remembered it, the question was whether IBM would be "building mediocrity" and opening the door to competitors.

A compelling argument in favor of introducing a compatible line of computers was that such a move would relieve IBM of the financial burden inherent in designing and servicing a host of incompatible machines. As things stood, the company was spending most of its development resources on a variety of CPUs, giving both programming and peripherals short shrift; with those parts of a system operating at suboptimal levels, no system's potential could be fully realized.

The committee presented its conclusions to IBM's top management in early January 1962. "Management listened to the report," Evans recalled, "accepted it, and we were all charged with the implementation plans the study had recommended." Thus was born the System/360, a stroke of entrepreneur-

Thomas Watson Jr., chairman of IBM *(near right)*, and company president T. Vincent Learson share the stage with a machine from the System/360 line, one of the biggest gambles in the history of the computer industry. A family of machines designed so that all of its members could run the same software and connect to the same input/output devices, System/360 debuted in April 1964, bringing with it the prospect of obsolescence for the rest of IBM's computers.

ial risk-taking altogether out of keeping with the company's past behavior.

System/360's technology was every bit the milestone Watson had implied, not least because its family-wide compatibility gave corporate computer users a new range of flexibility. Before System/360, corporations had been locked into package deals, configurations of hardware and software developed by the computer manufacturer. Now business users could piece together equipment and software appropriate to their own needs. Perhaps of most significance to corporate data-processing departments was the prospect of being able to add or substitute components to meet changing requirements without having to shut down the entire system for reprogramming.

IBM's tremendous clout in the marketplace gave System/360 a long reach: It created the so-called plug-compatible industry. Other manufacturers quickly realized that in a modular computer system whose components conformed to a common standard, not all the modules have to come from the same company. Sensing big profits, they rushed to make devices that would work with System/360 computers. Such non-IBM devices were said to be plug-compatible: They required no special programming or other adjustments but could simply be plugged in to begin communicating with IBM machines (or with any other plug-compatibles). Just as IBM could now afford to serve its customers better by making peripherals and software as efficient as possible, other companies could afford to mass-produce plug-compatibles for what would rapidly become the industry's leading line.

A NEW AGE OF FLEXIBILITY

With System/360, IBM had led the industry into a new, more freewheeling era in input/output technology. During the 1960s and 1970s plug-compatible manufacturers proliferated to such an extent that the company lost 13 percent of the peripherals market for its own computers to these competitors. Yet such was the scope of System/360's success that the absolute dollar volume of IBM's business continued to grow at a handsome rate, and the company's prominence in the computer industry became greater than ever. Even 20 years later, more than half of IBM's gross income and earnings could be attributed to the direct descendants of System/360.

Even as IBM's turn to standardization created unprecedented flexibility for corporate computer users, a new order of flexibility for individuals was in the making. The early 1960s were an especially fruitful time in the world of computer research projects funded by noncommercial sources. A particularly generous funder was the Pentagon's Advanced Research Projects Agency (ARPA), flush with money appropriated by Congress in the nervous years following the Soviet Union's launch of *Sputnik* in 1957. Recipients of ARPA funds did not have to stick to applied, or so-called bread-and-butter, research; they were free to devote their energies to the purely speculative kind of projects known as "blue sky."

One blue-sky group that benefited from ARPA's largess was the Augmentation Research Center (ARC) in Menlo Park, California. ARC was a small unit within the Stanford Research Institute (SRI), a think tank then sponsored by Stanford University. From the early 1960s into the beginning of the next decade, computer scientists at ARC generated enough breakthroughs to keep the computer industry busy for years.

THE BEGINNING OF A LONG CRUSADE
ARC got its name from founder Douglas Engelbart's fascination with what he called "human augmentation technology"—that is, the idea that computers should enhance human performance. Engelbart had been introduced to electronics while serving as a naval radar technician in World War II. After the war, he took a job with a California contractor for the National Advisory Committee on Aeronautics, a forerunner of the National Aeronautics and Space Administration. In 1951, he quit to pursue a doctorate in electrical engineering at the University of California at Berkeley.

Even in those days, when engineering students worked with computers that occupied entire rooms, Engelbart was musing aloud about such unheard-of things as using the machines as teaching tools and hooking them up to devices that would let people interact with them in new ways. "When I first heard about computers," he recalled later, "I understood, from my radar experience, that if these machines can show you information on punch cards and print-outs on paper, they could write or draw that information on a screen." Years before the technology was widely available, Engelbart outlined a system in which computers could display symbols on a cathode-ray tube. It was the beginning of what would prove to be a long crusade.

In 1957, Engelbart accepted a job at SRI. A year and a half later, he persuaded the institute to establish ARC and managed to obtain a small grant from the U.S. Air Force Office of Scientific Research. For the next few years, ARC could not afford additional staff, and Engelbart toiled in virtual isolation. "It was lonely work, not having anybody to bounce these ideas off," he said. In 1963, he outlined some of those ideas in a paper titled "A Conceptual Framework for the Augmentation of Man's Intellect"—a declaration of his technological creed and a wish list of concepts to explore at ARC.

As an example of an activity that could benefit from high-powered electronic aids, Engelbart chose writing, defining it as a task that involves multiple levels of intellectual ability. At the bottom of the hierarchy is the simple mechanical act of fingering the keyboard to make letters appear; at the top are tasks such as imagining, organizing and structuring the writing. More than 15 years before word processors became common tools, Engelbart envisioned a writing machine that

Dwarfed by an image of his own face, computer scientist Douglas Engelbart conducts a reprise of a show he first put on at the 1968 Fall Joint Computer Conference in San Francisco. There he stunned the audience with a demonstration of devices that made communicating with a computer simpler and more flexible than it had ever been before. His console (above) included an ordinary keyboard for entering text, a separate set of keys for issuing commands and a pointing device called a mouse for selecting items on the screen.

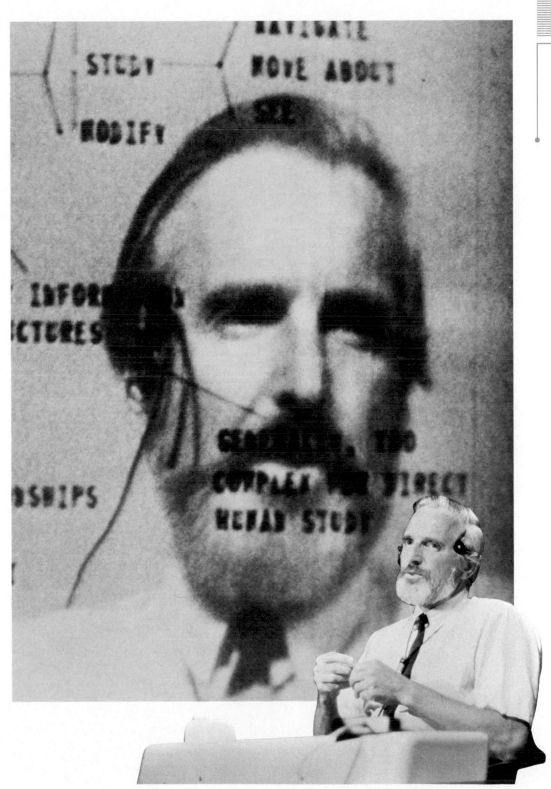

would automate the work at the bottom of the hierarchy, freeing the writer to do more and better work at the top. "For instance," he wrote, "trial drafts can be rapidly composed from rearranged excerpts of old drafts, together with new words or passages which you insert by hand typing."

Engelbart also elaborated on a theoretical system for manipulating symbols and images. "This could be a computer with which individuals could communicate rapidly and easily," he wrote, "coupled to a three-dimensional color display within which *extremely sophisticated images* could be constructed, the computer being able to execute a wide variety of processes on parts or all of these images in automatic response to human direction."

Engelbart's concepts met with resounding silence from most of the computer science community. But one man who shared his vision was Robert Taylor, funding director for the Information Processing Techniques Office at ARPA. In 1964, Taylor offered SRI and ARC an annual grant of half a million dollars to support augmentation research. Engelbart could finally put his theories into practice. For the next four years, assisted by a succession of gifted researchers, he dreamed and experimented, building and testing new devices and systems. Then, in 1968, he was invited to speak at a major computer conference scheduled to be held in San Francisco that fall. Engelbart decided to take the opportunity to demonstrate what he had been preaching for nearly 20 years.

By 1973, researchers at Xerox Corporation's Palo Alto Research Center (PARC) were employing a versatile paint program to turn their computer screens into electronic canvases. With the aid of an electronic pen, users could select a color from the palette at the top of the screen and a brush from the shapes on the left.

A MULTIMEDIA HAPPENING

People who witnessed the event describe it in terms more commonly applied to rock concerts and light shows than to presentations by computer scientists. Computer graphics pioneer Andries van Dam of Brown University called it "mind blowing." In fact, the demonstration was a multimedia production, requiring the behind-the-scenes efforts of a crew of video and telecommunications technicians. Seated at an unusual-looking console on the stage of the San Francisco Civic Auditorium, Engelbart wore a headset similar to those used by jet pilots. He addressed the audience by means of the mouthpiece microphone while listening through the earphones to the cross talk of the production crew. A microwave antenna set up in the hills above Menlo Park connected his control panel and screen to the host computer at the ARC lab 40 miles away. While his televised image loomed on a 20-foot screen behind him, Engelbart and a partner seated at a second set of controls at the ARC lab took turns conjuring up sample computerized documents, which moved on and off the big screen, superimposed over Engelbart's face.

Members of the audience, whether they realized it or not, were watching the future in action. Although the hardware used in the demonstration was makeshift and imperfect, Engelbart's vision of interactive computing came alive that day. The audience could sense the ease with which the two operators manipulated images, altered text and moved nimbly among the data files stored in the computer's memory. For years, Engelbart had been trying to explain his dream in words. That day in San Francisco, he stopped explaining and just put on a show.

From time to time during the demonstration, the background image of Engelbart's face would give way to views of his hands working the computer system's controls. With one hand, he operated something he called a chord keyset, an input device that resembled a five-key segment cut from a piano's keyboard. With the other, he rolled and clicked a gadget about the size of a pack of playing cards; it moved on hidden wheels and had a pair of buttons on top and a cable connection to the console. Technically known as an "x-y position indicator for a display system," it was something Engelbart had invented four years earlier and had named—because of its small size and tail-like cable—a mouse. With the mouse (and his audience) in the palm of his hand, Engelbart caused an electronic pointer to move around on the screen; the click of a button would compel whole paragraphs to shift position. Clearly, this was a type of human-machine interaction totally different from what was possible with the more conventional keyboard.

At the end of the 90-minute show, the audience gave Engelbart a standing ovation. And yet, as happened with virtually all of Engelbart's ideas, the recognition of the marketplace came much later—and to others.

By the early 1970s, growing opposition to the Vietnam War was making all U.S. defense spending increasingly controversial. Finally, in 1975, ARPA cut off Engelbart's funds. The ARC staff dwindled from a high of 35 to a dozen and then to one—Engelbart, working alone again. Two years later, Engelbart had left.

In some ways, ARC had served as a way station between the business-oriented culture of the mainframe computer world and the more adventuresome and humanistic culture of personal computing that emerged in the late 1970s. The computers Engelbart had worked with at ARC were too big and expensive for individuals to own. But the new concepts in hardware and software that had been born in his lab pushed computer science into its next stage of development.

The informality of group sessions such as this one was characteristic of the atmosphere at Xerox PARC in the early 1970s. Beanbags were seen as conducive to brainstorming—and some researchers even substituted the giant cushions for visitors' chairs in their offices.

Tools for Moving the Cursor

Much of the interaction between computers and human operators centers on a flashing marker, or cursor, that appears on a computer's video screen. The cursor indicates where the next action will be displayed and moves in response to commands from the keyboard. For example, typing a character moves the cursor one position to the right; striking one of the specially designated cursor keys can move the marker in one of four directions—up, down, left or right. This scheme is adequate for many computer applications, but when the cursor must be moved more than one or two positions at a time, or when greater flexibility of movement is desired—as in games, for example—cursor keys are slow and clumsy. Presented here and on the next two pages are some alternatives to cursor keys—devices designed to let users move the cursor more freely around the screen.

The most widely used alternative pointing device is the mouse (*below*), held in the hand and pushed along a flat surface. It will move the cursor in any direction on the screen. Mice come in two basic versions, optical (*top right*) and mechanical (*bottom right*). Buttons on the housing allow the user to select a command from a displayed menu, for example, or determine the end point of a line drawn on the screen.

Moving a mouse across a flat surface causes the cursor to travel in a corresponding direction on the screen (*below*). The speed and scale of mouse-to-cursor movement can be adjusted through software. If the mouse runs out of surface area before the cursor has moved sufficiently in a particular direction, the user may return the mouse to its starting point and roll it back over the same area to achieve additional movement of the cursor.

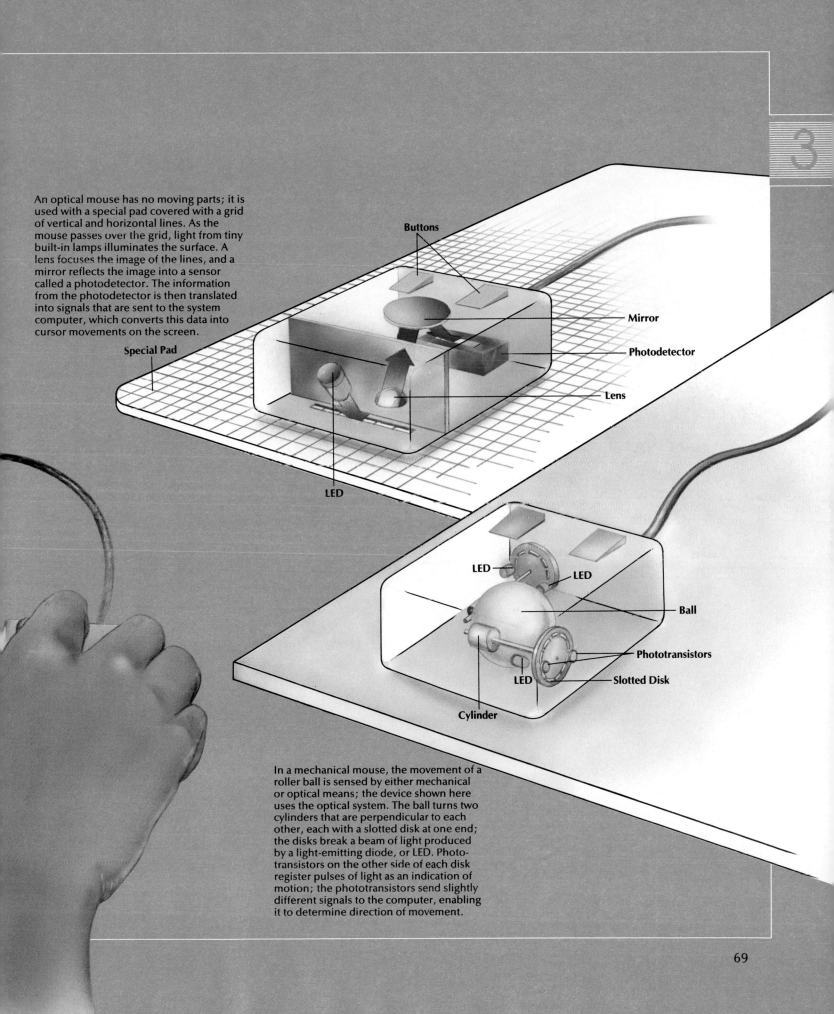

An optical mouse has no moving parts; it is used with a special pad covered with a grid of vertical and horizontal lines. As the mouse passes over the grid, light from tiny built-in lamps illuminates the surface. A lens focuses the image of the lines, and a mirror reflects the image into a sensor called a photodetector. The information from the photodetector is then translated into signals that are sent to the system computer, which converts this data into cursor movements on the screen.

Special Pad

Buttons

Mirror

Photodetector

Lens

LED

LED

LED

LED

Ball

Phototransistors

Slotted Disk

Cylinder

In a mechanical mouse, the movement of a roller ball is sensed by either mechanical or optical means; the device shown here uses the optical system. The ball turns two cylinders that are perpendicular to each other, each with a slotted disk at one end; the disks break a beam of light produced by a light-emitting diode, or LED. Photo-transistors on the other side of each disk register pulses of light as an indication of motion; the phototransistors send slightly different signals to the computer, enabling it to determine direction of movement.

A Gallery of Game Controllers

Devices often used as controllers for games and graphics include thumbwheels, joysticks and trackballs. Thumbwheels, which move the cursor in either direction along one axis, are used in pairs to propel the cursor anywhere on the screen. Early digital joysticks moved the cursor in as many as eight directions; newer digital models maneuver it in any direction, as do analog joysticks and trackballs.

A cursor's position at the end of a move depends on whether or not the controller's range of motion bears an absolute correspondence to the area of the screen. With an absolute joystick, for example, moving the stick to its lower left position moves the cursor to the screen's lower left; with a so-called rate joystick, however, pushing the stick to the left moves the cursor to the left of where it was, but not to a particular spot on the screen. Absolute devices are thus more effective for rapid, gross movement of the cursor; rate devices give finer control. Some devices can be switched from one mode to the other.

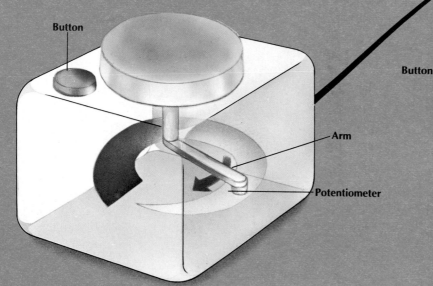

Button

Arm

Potentiometer

Button

Contacts

Button

Most thumbwheels work much like the volume knob on a radio. An arm inside the housing sweeps along a potentiometer, which measures changes in voltage and determines both the speed and the direction of the cursor. A button on the outside of the housing can be used to execute commands.

This early digital joystick is mounted on crossed bars with electrical contacts at four end points. When the stick is moved in an east-west or north-south direction, it makes contact with a given end point, and the cursor moves in one of the four primary directions. To move the cursor in intermediate directions requires pointing the stick midway between two end points; this causes both bars to make contact. Buttons for executing commands may be located on the joystick or on the housing.

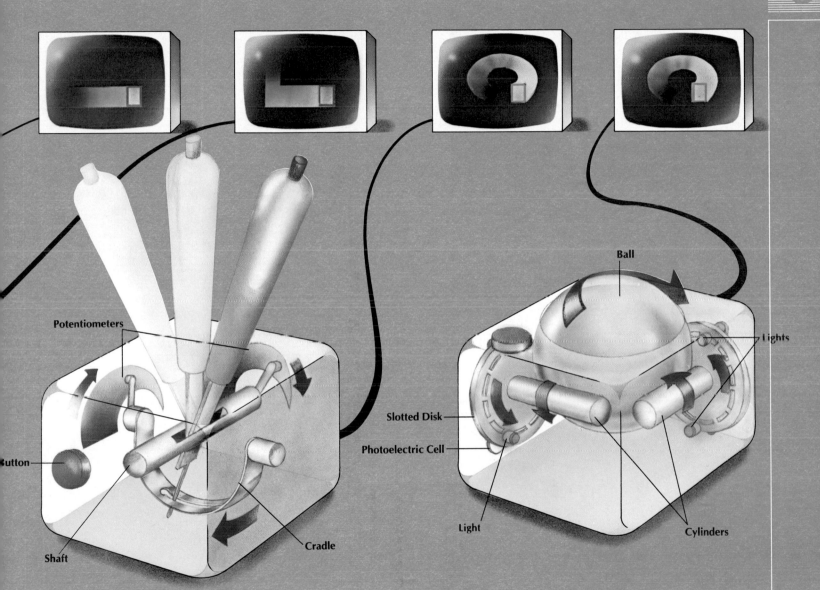

Potentiometers

Button

Shaft

Cradle

Ball

Lights

Slotted Disk

Photoelectric Cell

Light

Cylinders

The base of this analog joystick descends through the shaft of one potentiometer and the cradle of another, arranged at right angles; one potentiometer registers vertical movement, the other horizontal. As the joystick moves, the top shaft may roll in one direction while the bottom cradle swings in the other. The computer samples the varying voltage received from each potentiometer and translates that information into movement of the cursor on the screen.

A trackball works very much like the mechanical mouse on page 69. But instead of rolling the trackball along a surface, the user rolls it in place—as if the mouse were turned upside down. Slotted disks at the ends of two cylinders interrupt two light beams. A photoelectric cell senses the resulting pulses of light and relays the information to the computer.

In a sketch by computer visionary Alan Kay, two children play with tablets representing the Dynabook, Kay's concept of the ultimate personal computer. Dynabook was meant to replace paper, pencils and even books.

Many of the innovations that reached a wide market with personal computers can be traced back to ARC by way of another institution located nearby. Founded in 1970 by the Xerox Corporation, the Palo Alto Research Center (PARC) attracted many of the brightest of Engelbart's former staff and forged dramatically ahead in some of the areas these researchers had opened up.

GENEROUS CORPORATE COFFERS

Xerox established PARC as a think tank with commercial goals—but goals that lay far off in the future. Flush from the success of its line of photocopiers, the company gave PARC a lot of money and a long leash, expecting it to perform research that would yield profits in about 10 years. To help run the computer science lab at PARC, Xerox tapped Bob Taylor, the ARPA official who had funded Engelbart's work at ARC and who had shown a consistent knack for spotting talent among young computer scientists. With his new sponsor's corporate treasury to back him up, Taylor was able to lure a world-class team to PARC's elegant accommodations on a hill overlooking Stanford University. One researcher on the staff boasted that, of the top 100 computer scientists in the world, 58 worked at PARC.

The author of that brash claim was an intellectual whirlwind named Alan Kay. The son of an artist mother and a research physiologist father, Kay learned to read at the age of two and a half and later narrowly missed making the national Quiz Kids radio program. For all his intelligence, Kay was an indifferent student, applying himself only to things he was interested in. At 15 he discovered music, and until computers came along a decade later to claim an equal share of his energies, music ruled his life.

A stint in the U.S. Air Force introduced Kay to computers and turned him into a crack programmer. After leaving the service, Kay studied mathematics and biology at the University of Colorado and then applied to do graduate work under computer graphics pioneer David Evans at the University of Utah. Evans took a chance on him. "His grades were poor and he was a very unimpressive student," Evans said later. "But he had done interesting things in theater and television and was a musician. I thought he'd be an interesting person to have around the lab.''

When Kay arrived at Utah in the fall of 1966, Evans handed him a thesis written a few years earlier by a brilliant M.I.T. graduate student named Ivan Sutherland. The thesis described a program called Sketchpad, which turned the computer into the electronic equivalent of an artist's pencil and paper. Sketchpad opened Kay's eyes to the computer's potential, not only for graphics but for a one-to-one kind of interaction that he was to pursue for the next 10 years.

THE LESSONS OF FLEX AND LOGO

At Utah, Kay quickly made a name for himself as a creative thinker. His thesis consisted of writing a language and software for Flex, a machine whose hardware was designed by another student. Kay's software made Flex, in effect, a prototype personal computer; but the machine never became a commercial product, largely because Kay's system required users to master very complicated commands. It was a lesson Kay would not forget.

In the course of his doctoral studies, Kay also came across the work of M.I.T.'s Seymour Papert, whose computer language LOGO used interactive graphics to help teach children to program. Like Flex, LOGO would have a lasting influence on Kay's thinking as he developed his notion of what a computer should be. By 1969—nearly eight years before personal computers penetrated the general marketplace—Kay had made up his mind that any system he designed would be powerful enough to stand alone as a personal computer, yet simple enough for children to use.

Upon getting his degree in 1969, Kay left Utah to work at Stanford's Artificial Intelligence Laboratory. By 1971, he had migrated down the road to Xerox PARC, attracted by its offer of near-perfect creative freedom: no urgent marketing demands, no undergraduates to teach. PARC cherished an image as a utopian community of thinkers. Nobody had to punch a time clock, but scientists put in 60- and 70-hour work weeks, and fanatical devotion to the various research projects went hand in hand with spectacular creativity.

Kay's team at PARC, the Learning Research Group, never numbered more than a dozen or so in the 10 years he stayed at the center. In that time, Kay's theoretical personal computer took more definite shape and found a name: Dynabook. It was to be no bigger than a student's notebook; it would have sophisticated text and graphics capabilities; and it would be a communication device that linked the user with all of the data bases and libraries in the world. The magic of Dynabook would be accessible, like the telephone or television, to anyone who wanted it. That meant a low price—around $500, Kay figured—and ease of use.

Ever since his experience with Flex back in Utah, Kay had held firm in the belief that computers should be controlled by some technique simpler than typing the commands on a keyboard. Like Doug Engelbart, whose astonishing demonstration in San Francisco he had witnessed, Kay wanted the ability to initiate powerful sets of computer instructions with elementary actions such as pointing to commands or items on the screen. Kay was determined that people be able to concentrate on the job at hand rather than on the commands needed to get the computer to respond. ''If a person has to thumb a manual to use the user interface, you have failed,'' he once declared.

Dynabook was a concept of such ambition that it taxed even PARC's facilities and highly motivated staff. The nearest thing Kay ever saw to a working model of his dream device was the Alto—or interim Dynabook, as he called it: a small computer made possible by the introduction of the microprocessor in late 1971.

The key to the Alto's prowess was Smalltalk, a visually oriented programming language that Kay wrote in 1972. Designed for use with a mouse (a notion the PARC group borrowed from Engelbart), Smalltalk enabled the Alto to display multiple documents and graphic images in windows, or partitioned sections, of its high-resolution screen. And instead of having to remember a lot of esoteric commands, users could simply call up a menu, or list of commands, and choose one by pointing to it with the mouse. Later, PARC introduced the notion of icons, or graphic representations of commands and processes. For example, in a modification of Smalltalk geared for business, users could begin typing or editing a document by pointing to an icon consisting of a sheet of paper in a file folder. By allowing pictures to take over some of the communication tasks that had previously been the exclusive territory of text and numbers, Smalltalk made the Alto not only very versatile but also easy for novices to use.

AN UNPURSUED OPPORTUNITY
Born two years before the announcement of the Altair in 1975, the Alto ranks as a contender for the title of world's first personal computer. But Xerox never tried to mass-produce the machine, thinking that there was not a large enough market. Instead, it built only 2,000, mostly for internal use; later, a few more went to highly placed government customers, some in Congress and the White House. Kay himself could not believe that anything less powerful than the Dynabook of his dreams would sell in significant numbers. "What I completely misunderstood about the microcomputer industry," he later admitted, "was the hunger people had for any kind of computer."

Not until 1977 did Xerox begin the process of marketing Alto technology. In 1981, the company released the Star 8010, an Alto-like computer designed to be able to depict a business desktop, using icons for familiar office objects such as documents, file cabinets and wastebaskets. But the Star's $16,000 price tag was a strong deterrent despite the machine's graphics razzle-dazzle, and sales were disappointing. By 1980, even before the Star hit the market, PARC pioneers were starting to drift away. Kay went off to Atari Corporation, which was just entering the computer market after reaping immense profits from the video games that made the joystick a fixture in thousands of homes. Many of his former colleagues were drawn to Apple Computer Company of Cupertino, California.

In 1979, as Apple was beginning work on a new office computer, a team headed by Apple cofounder Steven Jobs had visited PARC and been given a demonstration of the Alto and Smalltalk's capabilities. Deeply impressed, Jobs and his colleagues promptly incorporated what they had seen into machines already on Apple's drawing board. Just as PARC had attracted Engelbart's ARC staff a decade earlier, Apple now lured away 15 to 20 Xerox scientists to work on Lisa, as their hot new computer was named.

With its multiple windows and its mouse- and icon-based user interface, Lisa's Xerox PARC origins were readily apparent. It reached the marketplace in 1983, but at $10,000, it was not a runaway success. Jobs soon realized that Lisa's price tag would put its exciting technology out of the reach of most potential users, so

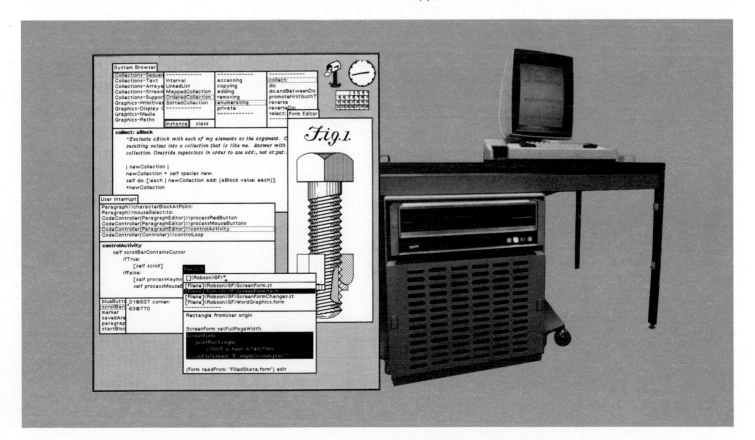

he turned to the development of a mouse-based, graphics-oriented computer for the masses: the Macintosh.

Apple introduced the new machine in early 1984 with a lavish campaign. "Since computers are so smart," the ads' theme ran, "wouldn't it make sense to teach computers about people instead of teaching people about computers?"

The Mac, as its followers quickly nicknamed it, was an instant hit; 275,000 were sold within nine months. Admirers lauded Apple for its vision in employing the new input/output techniques that gave the Mac its flexibility. Of course, as Kay and others pointed out, all of these techniques had been around for some time. But the Mac's arrival turned the computer industry upside down. People who owned other computers coveted the Mac's graphics and simplicity. Software that allowed other manufacturers' machines to use windows and mice quickly became hot sellers.

It had taken 20 years, but the seeds of a fundamental change in human-machine interaction that had been planted by Douglas Engelbart and nourished by Alan Kay and Xerox PARC were finally coming to fruition. Yet just as the advent of keyboards and screens could not presage the development of multiple windows or the mouse or the joystick, neither can these predict the ways humans and computers will interact in the future. "The Dynabook will be the last stage of computers as an object," Kay has said of his pet machine. "The next stage of the machines is for them to disappear."

The Alto, a stand-alone computer developed in 1973 at Xerox PARC, embodied many of Alan Kay's Dynabook concepts, but it was far too bulky and expensive for his purposes. Still, thanks to Kay's Smalltalk language, the Alto could display text and high-resolution graphics in multiple windows (inset), and the user could initiate commands simply by selecting icons on the screen with a mouse.

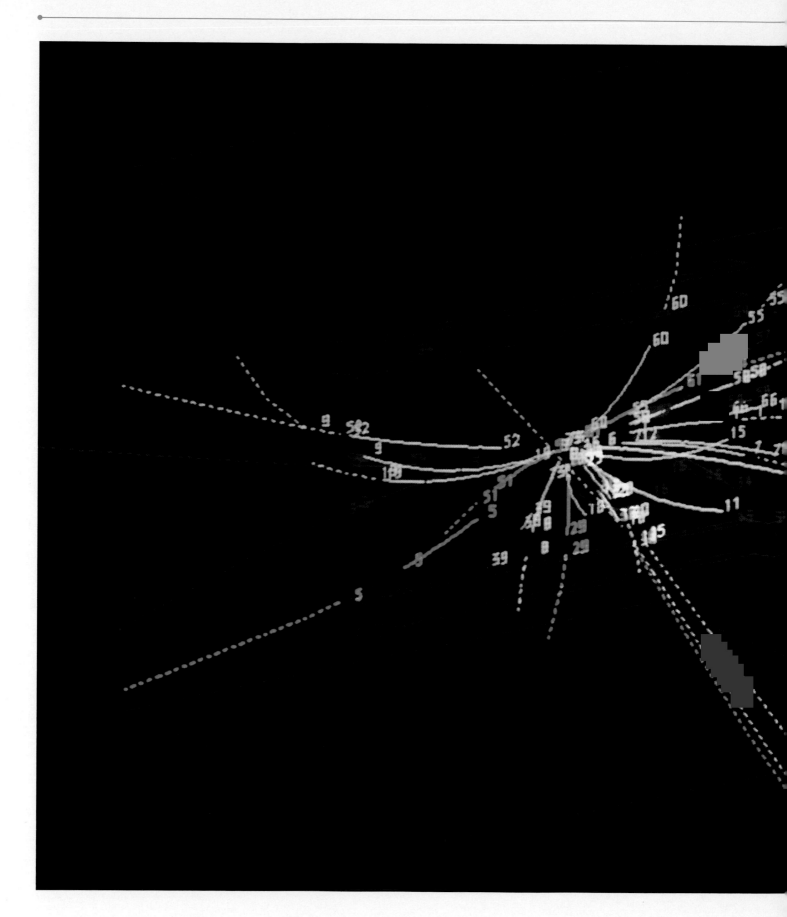

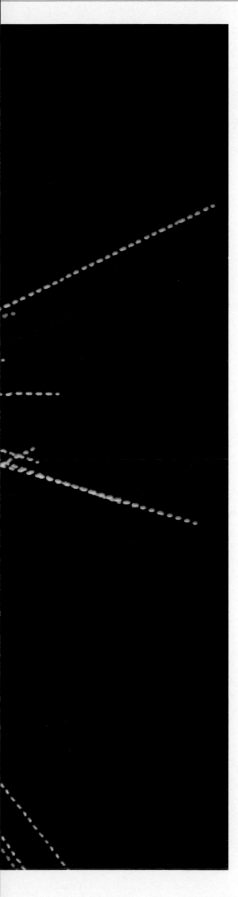

Of Medicine, Machines and Other Marvels

Dwarfed by the milling machine that nearly surrounds it, a foot-long titanium ingot slowly acquires a new shape, transformed by a spinning cutter that moves across its surface, spewing shavings. Then, in a stately mechanical minuet, the cutter pulls back and shifts to a new position while the ingot revolves to present another surface to be sculpted. All these movements are orchestrated by a computer; the finished product will be one of the more exotic forms of computer output: a custom-made artificial hip joint.

Traditionally, the creation of artificial joints and other prosthetic devices has been accomplished either entirely or partly by hand. Many commonly used prostheses are mass-produced in a variety of standard sizes, but these require tailoring. If X-rays indicate, for example, that a standard artificial knee joint needs to be shortened to fit the patient, a technician grinds the joint to the proper dimensions prior to surgery. All too often, however, the fit proves flawed, and additional modifications have to be made by the attending surgeon.

Computers can do away with the manual phase of this process and, more important, eliminate its hit-or-miss nature. First, a precise representation of the shape of the joint to be replaced is generated by a CAT (computerized axial tomography) scanner. This massive, doughnut-shaped device emits X-rays as it rotates around a section of the body. The X-rays are not recorded on film; instead, special detectors measure the intensity of each beam as it passes through the body and forward the information to a computer, which organizes the readings into a three-dimensional image of the affected area.

All the data used to compose this image is fed into a computerized design system. This system lets the designer—usually a biomedical engineer, in consultation with the surgeon—see the image from the CAT scan on a video screen and compare it with models of standard prostheses stored in the computer's memory.

The collision of a proton and an antiproton, as shown in this computer reconstruction of a high-energy physics experiment, produces pairs of lighter particles that fly off in opposite directions. But there are no opposing twins for the particles indicated by the three blue streams in the foreground; the mystery may imply the existence of new particles or forces. To conduct this kind of research, scientists employ sensitive detectors, which feed data to powerful computers.

The designer can use the computer to adapt one of the standard devices to the patient or to create an entirely new device to fit the patient's bone structure. In 15 minutes or less, the computer will produce drawings and specifications for the mechanical replacement, based on the tomographic data and on other factors, such as the patient's age and degree of physical infirmity. Approved by the surgeon and the engineer, the design is electronically transmitted to the milling machine. Then the surgery takes place—and a successful fit is usually ensured.

SYSTEMS FOUNDED ON I/O
The process that results in the titanium joint exemplifies the way computers have moved into realms very unlike the business office or research laboratory. Yet in so doing, the computer itself has often yielded pride of place to a host of sometimes unusual input and output devices. Instead of receiving data from card readers, keyboards or tape drives, computers may accept it from CAT scanners and other types of sensors. Similarly, computer output may bypass the conventional display of results on a screen or a paper print-out to guide precision tools, record results of experiments on the frontiers of physics, or control operations in large buildings. Moreover, these elaborate systems carry on with minimal human intervention, performing their jobs more consistently, more exactly and more efficiently than fallible humans could.

In many cases, the devices employed in highly automated systems have evolved from existing tools and systems. The computer-controlled apparatus that manufactures artificial joints, for instance, is a type of machine tool—a category of tool that also includes lathes, grinders, borers, drills and many other implements fundamental to manufacturing. Once, all machine tools required human operators to manipulate their controls. In the mid-1950s, however, the process was partially automated through the introduction of punched paper tape similar to that used by teletypewriter equipment and computers. The tape was prepared with coded instructions and fed to an automatic tape reader on the machine; the reading device then translated the code into mechanical actions necessary to produce a given part.

Specifications for each part thus were encoded and punched into the tape just once, and the tape could be stored for reuse later if more parts were needed; the result was a dramatic saving in production time and costs. For instance, a routine machining job that entailed drilling 100 evenly spaced holes once required eight hours to do by hand; with machines controlled by punched tape, the job could be completed in less than an hour.

In the 1960s, computer-aided design and manufacturing (CAD/CAM) systems brought production costs down even further. With CAD/CAM, an engineer could use graphics input devices such as light pens and trackballs (page 71) to create a detailed image of a part—a valve, a rotor or a turbine blade—on the computer's bit-mapped screen (pages 52-53). The computer could then use the data to draft a design for additional study or could translate the information into instructions for a machine tool.

By the early 1970s, computer-controlled machine tools were being linked to form more integrated flexible manufacturing systems (FMS). Most effective in factories that make a wide variety of products in relatively small quantities—an aircraft-parts factory, for example—FMS employs complementary machines that

In February 1959, the United States Air Force handed out dozens of aluminum ashtrays like this one, to demonstrate a manufacturing breakthrough. The ashtrays—the first objects ever produced with computer-aided design and manufacturing—were the product of a machine-tool programming language called APT developed by engineers at M.I.T.

are combined into groups called manufacturing cells. The cells can perform all the operations required to produce parts of similar design, however complex.

Typically, each machine in a manufacturing cell is controlled by a microcomputer; the micros are connected to a larger computer that coordinates the activities of the cell; these computers are in turn connected to a mainframe that oversees operations for the entire production line. The machines themselves are linked by a conveyor that carries pieces from one machine to the next.

In some systems, machines are equipped to check the accuracy of their own work. Special gauges monitor the shaping of each piece and relay the information to the machine's microcomputer. The computer compares incoming data with programmed standards and can adjust the machine instantly—and minutely—to correct deviations, thus eliminating the need for jigs to keep drilling and cutting tools properly aligned. With this level of control, the machine can cut metal to tolerances of $1/10,000$ of an inch. Moreover, an FMS factory can run day and night with a fraction of the personnel needed in a conventional plant. Once the pieces to be machined are loaded onto the conveyor belt, they move automatically from one manufacturing cell to another in proper sequence. Thus the system need be loaded and unloaded only once a day, requiring just one human monitor the rest of the time. With computer-controlled machines linked in an FMS, the portion of the workday that a machine spends actually cutting or shaping a part can be as high as 50 to 90 percent; stand-alone machines, even when controlled by computers, are active only 10 to 30 percent of the time.

QUICK ADJUSTMENTS TO THE MARKETPLACE

FMS has been called the ultimate entrepreneurial system, conferring on a manufacturer astounding responsiveness to market trends and the ability to expand, shrink or change a product line almost at will. In a shop without FMS, the manufacturer must shut down for several hours to modify or replace machines whenever retooling is necessary. With FMS, retooling for a new product means little more than changing the software that directs a manufacturing cell.

Ease of retooling lets a manufacturer customize a product to a degree that would once have been impossible. For example, an FMS factory operated by General Electric in Somersworth, New Hampshire, can turn out 2,000 versions of an electric meter to accommodate as many variations in the ways in which customers are billed or in the ways power is transmitted to their buildings.

Another aspect of FMS is the unprecedented control over inventory it bestows on a manufacturer. For example, Deere & Co., a maker of farm and industrial equipment, has computerized its tractor-assembly process so that particular combinations of engines, wheels and transmissions, for instance, can be assigned to tractors ordered by specific dealers. The parts are retrieved from storage and delivered to the assembly line just as they are needed, enabling Deere to maintain only a small inventory of completed tractors. Similarly, automobile manufacturers who were once obliged to maintain large inventories of spare parts for older models may now produce those parts as needed, virtually eliminating waste and storage costs.

Precision machine tools used in flexible manufacturing are an example of specialized output devices making up the major portion of a computer-controlled system. Elsewhere, input devices take the lead role. Specialized sensors,

Testing Reactions with Fast Feedback

A driver stepping into the test car at the Daimler-Benz research center in Berlin is entering an extremely sophisticated I/O device: a driving simulator. Using technology developed to train jet pilots, the German automobile company has surrounded the car with an illusory world of rainy highways and defiant pedestrians; as the driver steers, the illusion reacts, forming a closed loop of action and response. Engineers hope eventually to be able to design safer cars and roads by studying the interaction between driver and vehicle in situations too complex or dangerous to be reproduced in real life.

This extraordinary test vehicle is attached to the floor of a 24-foot-wide simulator dome mounted on six stiltlike hydraulic pistons. Six projectors on the dome's ceiling display a moving scene—say, a rural highway at night—onto a screen curving around the front half of the car. As the driver operates the vehicle, sensors linked to the steering and pedals send their data to a high-speed computer that calculates the changing dynamics of the situation in real time, solving 2,000 equations every 10 milliseconds. The results then travel to secondary computers controlling not only the image but sound effects such as squealing tires. These computers also dictate the motion of the dome itself, which swings and rolls on its hydraulic legs to create a realistic sensation of motion for the car's occupant. New images and sounds are broadcast back into the dome 50 times a second, so rapidly that most drivers discern no time lag.

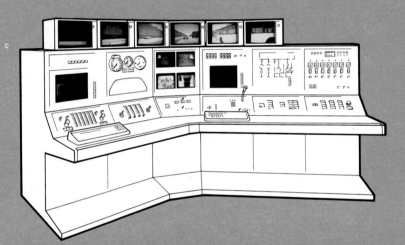

Control station
Operators directing the action of the simulator dome sit at a nearby control station (*left*). Six monitors at the top of the control station display the simulated scenes produced by six ceiling projectors, while video screens in the center show other portions of the action inside the room. Operators communicate with the computers through terminals on either side of the video screens. Test managers may alter the simulation using banks of keys and levers, changing the scene from sunlight to rain, for example, or stopping the test altogether.

Inside the simulator
The realism of the driving simulator (*left*) starts with a full-size Mercedes-Benz. The car's interior is complete, but its engine, transmission and axles have been replaced by sensors that record the movements of the steering wheel and brakes; hydraulic actuators replicate the normal resistance of steering and pedals. A computer-generated moving scene of a simulated roadway is projected onto a screen that encompasses the front half of the car. The only clue to the unreality of the situation is that the driver has no rear view.

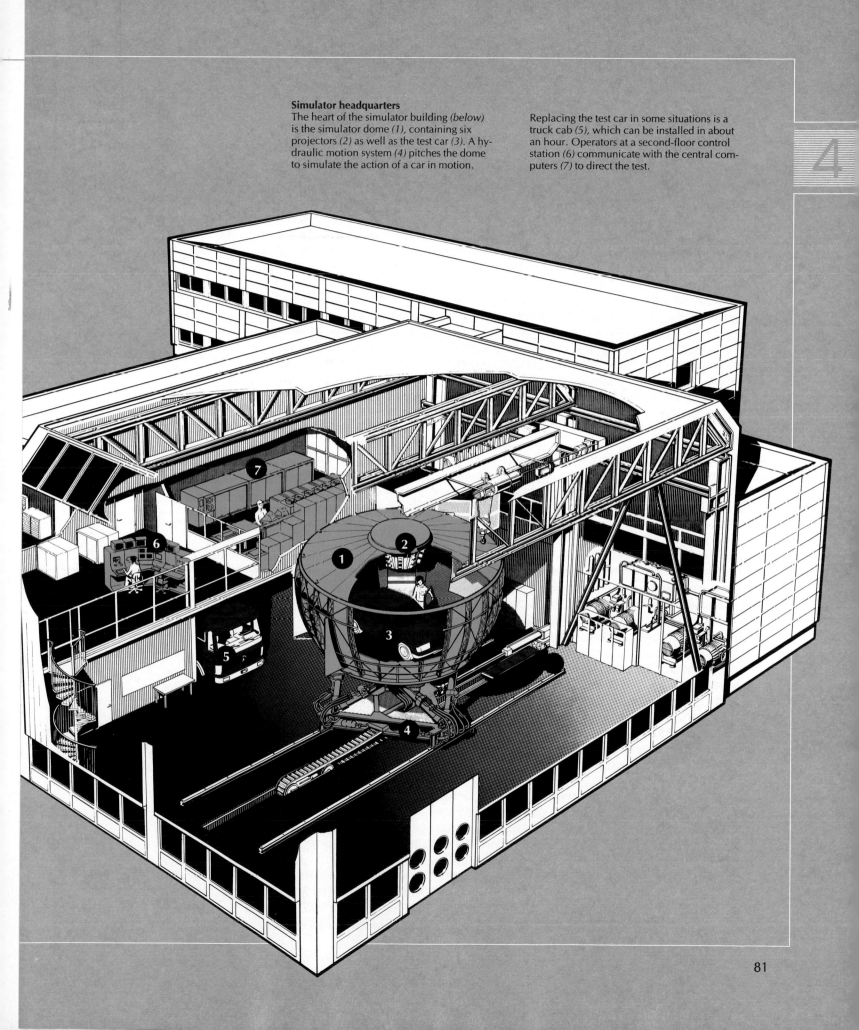

Simulator headquarters
The heart of the simulator building *(below)* is the simulator dome *(1)*, containing six projectors *(2)* as well as the test car *(3)*. A hydraulic motion system *(4)* pitches the dome to simulate the action of a car in motion.

Replacing the test car in some situations is a truck cab *(5)*, which can be installed in about an hour. Operators at a second-floor control station *(6)* communicate with the central computers *(7)* to direct the test.

accurate input from other sensors during launch. The critical nature of this information was made abundantly clear in July 1985, when, nearly six minutes into an apparently flawless launch, the space shuttle *Challenger* appeared to experience a failure in one of its three main engines.

High over the Atlantic Ocean and traveling 11,900 miles per hour, *Challenger* followed orders from the ground to "abort to orbit," a standard emergency procedure when a shuttle mission gets into trouble during launch. If so instructed, the crew attempts to continue spaceward, even if the orbit achieved is not the one originally intended. If the engine had shut down 33 seconds earlier, *Challenger* would have been unable to reach orbital velocity and would have had to land at an emergency strip in Zaragoza, Spain. By firing the two remaining engines 86 seconds longer than scheduled, and by getting an extra boost from a pair of smaller orbital-maneuvering engines, mission commander Gordon Fullerton pushed the shuttle into a path about 190 miles above the earth, 50 miles lower than planned. Although this position was less than optimum, *Challenger's* seven-person crew was able to carry out its scientific mission with no further orbiting problems, returning home eight days later with a wealth of astronomical data.

FINDING THE WEAK LINK
The mission's ultimate success could not obscure the fact that *Challenger* had sailed uncomfortably close to serious trouble. In 19 shuttle flights and a total of 50 manned flights in the history of the U.S. space program, this was the first time that a main engine had shut down prematurely. As a subsequent investigation showed, however, it was not the huge engine itself that had failed but heat sensors installed in the engine's gas manifold.

Each of the shuttle's three main engines is regulated by an individual computer. Linked as input devices to each of these computers are two heat sensors, or probes—thin wires in which electrical resistance increases with a rise in temperature. Should the engine overheat dangerously, the computer would respond by shutting it down. The sustained high temperatures in the gas manifold, however, can cause a probe to burn out and send a falsely high reading to the computer. To prevent the engine from being shut down by mistake, the computer is programmed to recognize the unreasonably high reading that characterizes a failed heat probe and disregard this erroneous data.

Engineers reconstructing events aboard *Challenger* concluded that one of the center engine's two probes failed decisively and the computer accordingly rejected its temperature reading. Then the second probe also failed, but in doing so it fooled the computer by sending a measurement that, while above the danger threshold of 1,390° F., was below the point the computer would recognize as unrealistic. The computer therefore accepted the reading as accurate, concluded that the engine was indeed overheating and shut it down three minutes early.

NASA engineers eliminated the problem on the next shuttle launch by using heat sensors made of a stronger alloy. Still, the incident underscores the fact that even the most sophisticated computer systems can do their jobs well only if they receive accurate information. In this case, GIGO—the computer world's acronym for Garbage In, Garbage Out—resulted in a near brush with disaster.

Flying with the Ultimate Copilot

Speed is a desirable quality in all computer systems, but in certain situations the near-instantaneous transfer of information from input to processor to output is a necessity. This high-velocity activity is called real-time computing. In modest form it is used in such applications as monitoring and coordinating manufacturing equipment to ensure efficiency. But perhaps the most challenging application of real-time computing, one in which a time lag could be fatal, is in the control of an experimental jet fighter that otherwise could not fly at all.

The supersonic X-29, unveiled by the Grumman Aerospace Corporation in 1984 (page 7), is distinguished by wings that sweep sharply forward toward the nose of the plane and by the absence of horizontal stabilizers on the tail. Just in front of the wings are a pair of winglike appendages called canards (from the French word for "duck"), which give the airplane additional lift. This radical design results in a degree of maneuverability no conventional fighter can match. The forward-swept wings also reduce drag, which means that the X-29 does not need as big an engine as does a conventional fighter of comparable performance.

But there is a trade-off. Flying the X-29 is roughly like shooting an arrow feathers first; the plane is wildly unstable. Airflow patterns around the unusual body give the X-29 a tendency to buck so violently that it could wrench itself apart in one fifth of a second. To counteract this destructive instability requires a continuous flow of as many as 40 adjustments per second to the canards and other exterior control surfaces — far more than even the best human pilot could execute.

As illustrated on the following pages, the human pilot of the X-29 is assisted by a real-time computer system. Guided by complex software, three digital computers monitor and control a network of highly sensitive input and output devices. The computers respond to changing flight conditions as fast as they occur, taking in sensor readings and sending out instructions that bring the X-29 back to stable flight even as the plane fights to deviate from it.

Anatomy of a Fail-Safe System

The system that keeps the X-29 aloft—and that prevents it from disintegrating—employs equipment in identical sets of three to do each job. This triple redundancy guarantees that no single malfunction will destroy the plane. At the heart of the scheme are three digital computers. If one fails, the other two will override its faulty instructions. In the unlikely event another one goes bad, three backup analog computers will take over. The analog machines do not provide optimum control, but they can bring the jet home in one piece.

Each digital computer receives input from its own set of sensors. The three computers compare this data, select the midlevel value for each type of sensor and process the values with software that provides formulas for any combination of input. The resulting commands are converted to analog signals. Because the precision of analog signals varies, only the midlevel signals are transmitted to the devices that manipulate the control surfaces. Despite its complexity, the X-29's system has performed well from the outset, both in thousands of hours of ground testing and simulation, and then in actual flight.

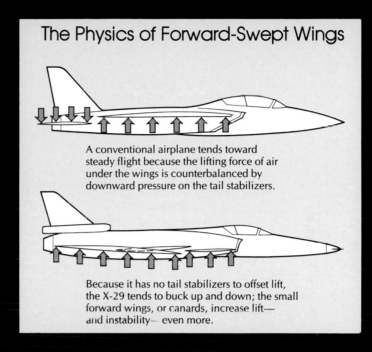

The Physics of Forward-Swept Wings

A conventional airplane tends toward steady flight because the lifting force of air under the wings is counterbalanced by downward pressure on the tail stabilizers.

Because it has no tail stabilizers to offset lift, the X-29 tends to buck up and down; the small forward wings, or canards, increase lift—and instability—even more.

The X-29's flight-control system is governed by three digital computers, which are connected to redundant input and output devices. Each computer has two microprocessors: One coordinates I/O, including pilot commands; the other runs software that determines precise output instructions.

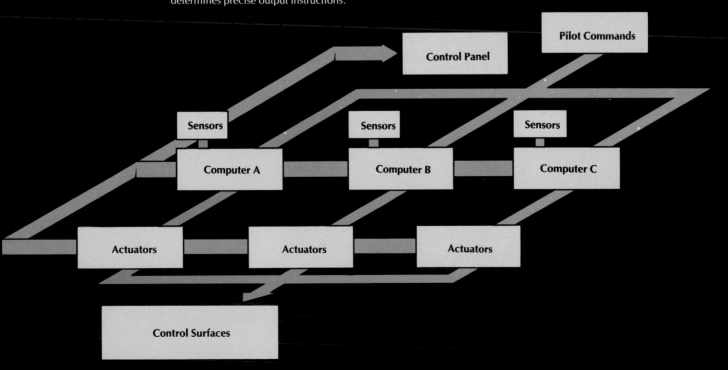

Gathering Data with a Network of Sensors

The job of monitoring the X-29's speed, angle of attack and other flight conditions belongs to sensors located at critical points along the plane's body. This network feeds data into the jet's three digital and three analog computers, which are located between the nose and the cockpit. Because they must detect real-world phenomena, most of the sensors are analog devices, producing continuous signals that vary with changing conditions.

Devices for sensing aerodynamic changes occupy leading positions. On the nose boom and on either side of the body are angle-of-attack vanes, which alter their orientation to match the airflow as the plane tilts up or down. On

Accelerometers

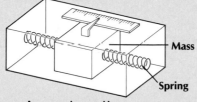

Measuring Acceleration

An accelerometer measures the rate at which speed changes. As the velocity of the aircraft increases or decreases, a calibrated mass inside the accelerometer exerts greater or lesser force against the springs that restrain it.

Measuring Motion along Three Axes

A rotating gyroscope resists any force that attempts to alter the orientation of its axis of spin (blue arrows). By analyzing the resistance detected by the yaw-, pitch- and roll-rate gyroscopes, the jet's computers determine the plane's rate of motion relative to its vertical, lateral and longitudinal axes.

the nose and sides of the plane are devices known as Pitot-static tubes, which gather air-pressure data used to calculate the plane's velocity.

In the wheel well beneath the wings are nine accelerometers, three each to measure the rate of change in longitudinal, lateral and vertical speed. Behind the pilot are 12 gyroscopes, six each to monitor the rates of yaw, or side-to-side sluing, and roll.

Six more gyroscopes measure pitch, or up-and-down bucking, the most important safety consideration on the X-29. In order to minimize possible distortion of the readings, the pitch-rate gyros are placed on the least flexible seg-

ment of the aircraft: the keel, just in front of the wheels.

The six gyros within each set are mounted inside the same casing to ensure that they give nearly identical readings. The casings are precisely machined to keep the gyros aligned with one another.

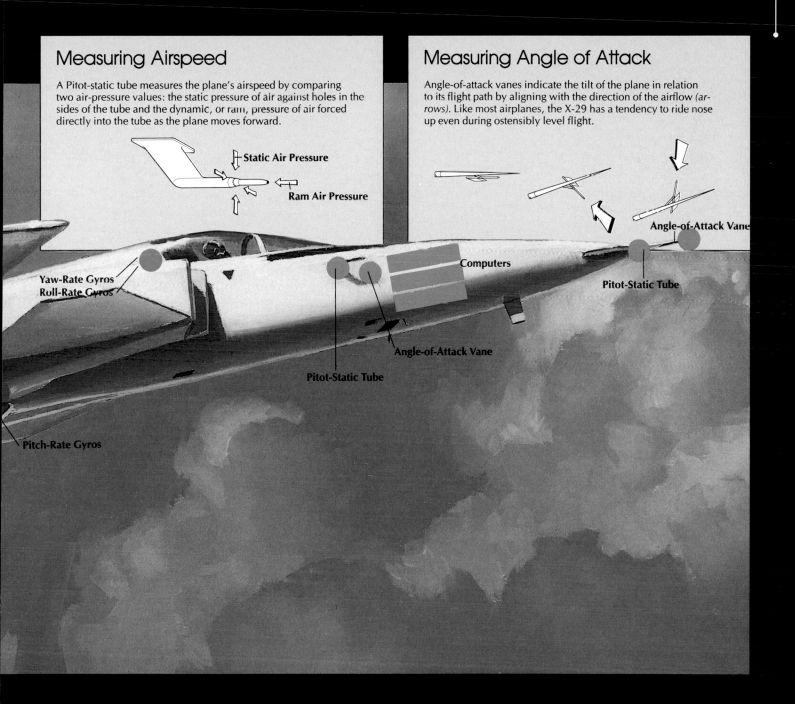

Measuring Airspeed

A Pitot-static tube measures the plane's airspeed by comparing two air-pressure values: the static pressure of air against holes in the sides of the tube and the dynamic, or ram, pressure of air forced directly into the tube as the plane moves forward.

Static Air Pressure

Ram Air Pressure

Measuring Angle of Attack

Angle-of-attack vanes indicate the tilt of the plane in relation to its flight path by aligning with the direction of the airflow (arrows). Like most airplanes, the X-29 has a tendency to ride nose up even during ostensibly level flight.

Angle-of-Attack Vane

Computers

Pitot-Static Tube

Yaw-Rate Gyros
Roll-Rate Gyros

Angle-of-Attack Vane

Pitot-Static Tube

Pitch-Rate Gyros

At the Controls of an Unstable Craft

A pilot seated at the controls of the X-29 finds a familiar environment: foot pedals to control yaw, a hand-operated joystick to change the pitch and roll of the plane, an instrument panel packed with assorted gauges and lights. At first glance, there is little to distinguish the X-29's cockpit from that of the less sophisticated F-5 fighter jet—and with good reason: The X-29's cockpit is taken from an F-5.

But beneath this familiar appearance lie some important differences. Like the gyroscopes and other I/O devices in the plane's control system, much of the cockpit equipment represents technology that has been used for years in conventional, mechanically controlled planes. Now, however, the technol-ogy has been adapted to the special requirements of the "fly-by-wire," or electronically controlled, X-29.

In a conventional fighter plane, the pilot manipulates the foot pedals and joystick, which have a direct mechanical link to the hydraulic devices that move external control surfaces such as the rudder and the wing flaps. In the X-29, however, the pilot's controls are computer-input devices, communicating only indirectly with the plane's steering equipment. Pushing on the joystick or stepping on the pedals conveys electronic signals that the computers read as input. The computers combine this cockpit input with data from all of the system's other sensors to calculate the needed adjustments.

A Panel Full of Warnings

The fail-status-control panel, a special area of the instrument panel known as the "pork chop" for its shape, is studded with warning lights to alert the pilot to malfunctions in the plane's I/O system. It also contains switches to neutralize the malfunctioning equipment. In the event of an equipment failure, the pilot can prepare for an immediate return to base while the redundant backup system continues to control the plane's stability.

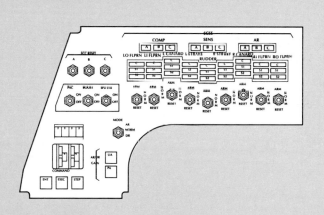

Regulating Pitch and Roll

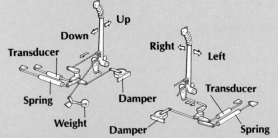

The joystick lets the pilot tilt the plane's nose up or down (pitch), or roll the craft to one side. But this control is indirect: Transducers turn stick movements into analog signals, which are converted to digital signals and sent to the computers. For the pilot's benefit, weights, dampers and springs re-create the feel of conventional controls.

Steering Left or Right

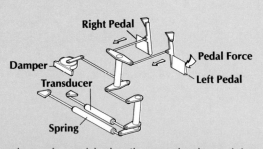

By working the two foot pedals, the pilot steers the plane to left or right (yaw). Like the joystick, the pedals send electronic signals to the computer while providing the pilot with mechanical feedback. The dampers and springs under the foot controls require the pilot to exert 40 to 50 pounds of pressure to depress the pedals.

Rapid-Fire Orders for ▮elicate Guidance

Forty times a second, the X-29's computers take in data, make their calculations and send out instructions. The result of this electronic labor is the mechanical action of the plane's control surfaces▮the rudder, atop the tail; the rear strakes, along either side of the tail; the flaperons, on the back edges of the wings; and the canards, behind the cockpit.

The control surfaces are moved by activator assemblies, which consist of pistons that are operated by hydraulic pressure regulated by control valves. Three control valves and a dual tandem hydraulic piston make up the activator assigned to each control surface. The control valves receive signals from the digital computers, check that all three computers have transmitted identical commands, then alter the hydraulic pressure on the pistons.

Each movable surface plays a different role in flying the X-29. The canards, for example, supplement the lift of the wings and are primarily responsible for controlling the pitch of the aircraft, while the strakes provide additional pitch contro▮The flaperons have several tasks: They combine the functions of wing flaps and ailerons, governing roll and providing additional lift, and they can also be used to reduce the camber▮or curvature, of the wings when the X-29 reaches supersonic speeds.

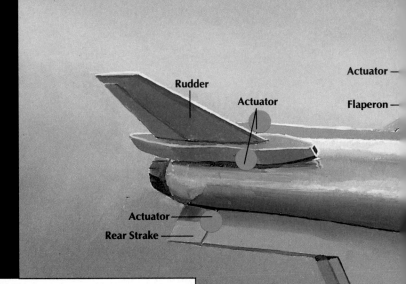

Rudder

Actuator

Actuator

Flaperon

Actuator

Rear Strake

Anatomy of the Plane's Hydraulic Muscles

Control valves in the activator assembly regulate the hydraulic pressure that makes a control surface move. Analog signals from the computers cause the valves to increase or decrease hydraulic pressure on the dual tandem piston. The piston, in turn, mechanically forces the appropriate control surface to change position.

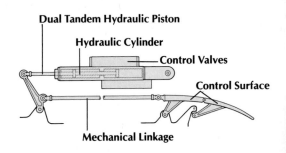

Dual Tandem Hydraulic Piston

Hydraulic Cylinder

Control Valves

Control Surface

Mechanical Linkage

Moving Surfaces That Keep the X-29 Aloft

The X-29's control surfaces include a conventional rudder, which steers the plane left or right; 30-inch rear strakes, which move up or down 30 degrees from center; double-hinged flaperons, which alter the curvature of the forward-swept wings; and the canards, which can rotate 30 degrees upward or 60 degrees down to control pitch and modify lift.

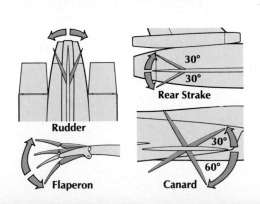

Rudder

Flaperon

30°

30°

Rear Strake

30°

60°

Canard

Actuator

Flaperon

Actuator

Canard

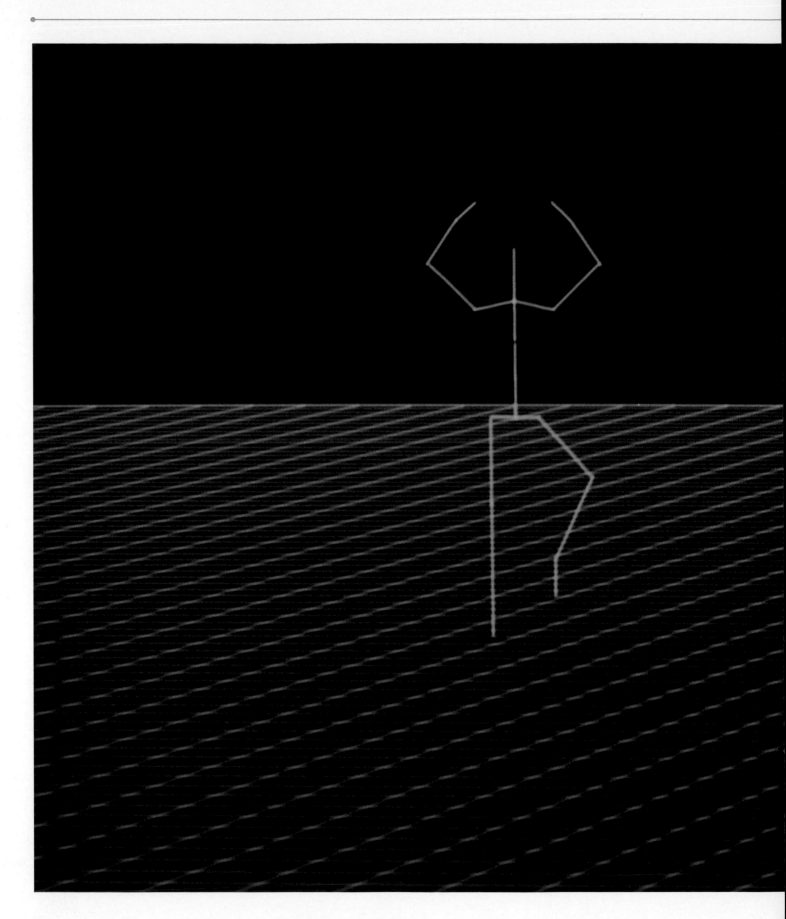

4

Transcending Limitations and Boundaries

There was nothing extraordinary about the fact that Rob Marince used a computer to dial his telephone, write letters and develop computer programs. All of these applications were increasingly common in the early 1980s when Marince began to learn how to work his Apple II. What made Marince's situation unusual were his system's provisions for input and output. Unable to move his arms or legs as the result of an automobile accident, Marince used his voice to communicate with his computer—and through it, with the world.

In 1977, at the age of 17, Marince had been thrown from a car into the path of an oncoming truck. Soon after the accident, his oldest brother, Gary, a radio broadcast engineer, began to piece together electronic hardware to give Rob a measure of independence. The first step was a whistle-activated control for both the television set and the telephone. In 1980, determined to give Rob more control over his environment and intrigued by advertising that touted Apple's machines as computers for everyone, Gary wrote to the Apple Computer Company and engaged the help of sympathetic engineers in putting together a system for Rob based on an Apple II Plus. The input device was a microphone connected to a sophisticated machine called a voice-entry terminal. This small box was a two-in-one instrument, part analog-to-digital converter, part microcomputer— and it was dedicated to the task of being Rob's alter ego. The terminal could break Rob's words down into the patterns of their component sounds, then look for similar patterns among approximately 200 commands stored in its memory. (Rob created the stored patterns, or templates, by repeating each command several times.) When the terminal found a match, it sent the computer a list of instructions for carrying out Rob's wishes. The output included sound-producing circuitry that synthesized speech so the computer could talk back to Rob, and controllers that could activate a number of other machines. At the center of the system was the personal computer, named HAL after the talking computer in the science-fiction novel and film *2001: A Space Odyssey*.

In a typical exchange, Rob might say, "Satellite search"; the computer would then respond: "What satellite do you want?" To Rob's command, "Satcom F3R,"

A stick figure's solitary dance heralds a new age of computer-assisted choreography—one of many fields enhanced by the computer's ability to transform virtually any form of input into almost any form of output. Choreographers hope to record their ephemeral art through more advanced versions of the animation program illustrated at left; such programs translate a dancer's motion into figures that move across a computer screen.

HAL would reply, "Yes, master." Behind the Marince home, a 13-foot dish antenna would swing into motion, sweeping the sky before stopping and focusing on a communications satellite orbiting 22,300 miles above the equator. "What transponder do you want?" the computer would then ask. "Atlanta," Rob might say, and moments later the TV at the foot of his bed would light up with a news broadcast from WTBS, a Georgia television station beamed via the satellite.

After about three years, Gary exchanged the Apple II Plus for a more powerful IBM XT, which could initiate action in response to Rob's commands almost twice as fast. Gary also traded the old voice-entry terminal for a more sophisticated model, and HAL's vocabulary jumped to more than 800 words. With the additional capacity, Rob could adjust the temperature of his bed, his room and even an aquarium; control his room's lights; operate a household intercom system; and activate an emergency power generator. He could also dictate letters, play video games and establish a link with the Carnegie-Mellon University computer network in nearby Pittsburgh to write computer programs. And at night, to keep from disturbing others in the house, Rob could instruct the machine to "change the pitch," causing HAL to respond in a whisper to all commands.

The system that keeps Rob Marince in touch with the world is one sophisticated example of the ways that computers—and the hardware and software of I/O—have been adapted to helping individuals do things that were previously impossible. The systems have allowed people to transcend the limits imposed by physical disabilities such as paralysis or blindness, and to go beyond the old boundaries of such disciplines as music and dance.

MASTERING MUSCULAR ACTION

In the early 1970s, Jerrold Petrofsky, a physiologist and biomedical engineer at St. Louis University in Missouri, was studying ways of inducing and controlling movement in paralyzed limbs. Stimulating muscular action was not hard; Luigi Galvani, an Italian scientist, had shown in the 18th century that electrical charges could produce movement in paralyzed muscles. Controlling that movement was another matter; even lifting a knee involves a complex interplay of muscular adjustments. Petrofsky designed a system of electrodes and sensors, connected to a computer, that could coordinate the firing of electrical impulses to activate leg muscles in simple sequences. Moving in 1979 to Ohio's Wright State University, he continued to work on his system; by 1982, it was ready to test with Nan Davis, a Wright State student paralyzed from the waist down in an auto accident the evening after her high-school graduation in 1978. He taped about 30 electrodes and sensors over the major muscle groups in Davis' legs. A desktop computer controlled the electrodes, which in early tests had stimulated the muscles so that Davis could pedal a stationary bicycle and regain muscle tone and strength.

Then Petrofsky and Davis began to work on walking. At one stage, the computer program called for a set of 2,721 instructions to be repeated 250 times each second. The sensors provided a feedback system, allowing the computer to monitor the movements of Davis' ankles, knees and hips so that it could make corrections to maintain her balance; the computer adjusted the voltages applied to the muscles 4,000 times each second. The resulting movements were crude and jerky, but the system worked. In 1983, Petrofsky slimmed down the 150-pound desktop system to a purse-size version, and at the university's graduation ceremonies, Davis was able to walk to the podium to receive her bachelor's degree in elementary education—and a standing ovation from the crowd of 8,000. It was the first time in five years that Davis had walked in public.

The computer-controlled muscle-stimulation system devised by Jerrold Petrofsky gave Nan Davis back the use of her legs. The voice-controlled alter ego that Gary Marince built for his brother enabled Rob Marince to manipulate the world around him even though he could not move at all. For others whose disabilities are not as immobilizing as those of Davis and Marince, computers with advanced I/O systems bestow the power to do slightly out-of-the-ordinary things that would otherwise be virtually impossible. Homer Page discovered this in 1978 when he decided to become a candidate for the Colorado legislature.

ON THE CAMPAIGN TRAIL
Page, an administrator of programs for students with disabilities, faced one enormous hurdle shared by few neophyte politicians: He was blind. But when voters asked him, as they frequently did, how he expected to read the vast amount of material necessary to keep current on legislative matters, he would tell them of a remarkable device that had helped transform his life.

The machine was about the size of an attaché case, and during the campaign Page used it to read hundreds of documents, from letters to legislation. He would place a document face down on the glass top of the unit, and a photoelectric sensor would scan the page line by line, converting the shapes of the characters into electrical signals. A small computer in the machine analyzed the signals to determine the identity of each letter, then grouped letters into words. Rules programmed into the machine determined how each word should be pronounced, and the computer would then activate a synthesizer (similar to the one that gave Rob Marince's HAL a voice) that could speak at the rate of 225 words per minute. Page could push a button to tell the machine to repeat or skip passages, or to mark a section of the page that he wished to read again later.

Page was narrowly defeated in his bid for office but decided to stay in politics anyway, having proved himself equal to the challenge. The reading machine that was his instrument of independence had also proved itself. By the early 1980s, it was beginning to appear in public libraries; people with impaired vision no longer needed someone else to read aloud printed material that had not been translated into braille or recorded on tape.

The reading machine was the brainchild of Raymond Kurzweil, a young engineer with an eclectic approach to the design of specialized input and output systems. The technology at the heart of the machine—which gave it the ability to read virtually any printed document—had its genesis during Kurzweil's days as an undergraduate at M.I.T. in the late 1960s. In a computer-science class there, he encountered a typically difficult problem in the field of artificial intelligence (AI): how to program a computer to perceive a common denominator when presented with different versions of the same thing. Pattern recognition, as AI researchers call this capacity, would, among other things, enable a computer to recognize the shapes of printed characters regardless of the typeface.

One system for character recognition had been around since the late 1950s, when banks began using magnetic ink character readers, or MICRs, to scan account numbers on personal checks. But MICRs could recognize only a highly stylized typeface. To be useful over a broader range of printed material, a reading device would need to recognize the approximately 300 different sizes and styles of type in common use, and not be fooled by different grades and colors of paper, by smudges and blots, by broken letters or letters that were connected.

Kurzweil was a budding entrepreneur (he had already developed a program to match high-school students with colleges, netting himself and a partner $100,000), and the commercial possibilities of a reading machine did not escape him. He kept the idea in mind while working as a software consultant after graduation in 1970, but a solution to the problem of pattern recognition did not come quickly. "It wasn't something that I developed in a flash in the shower or in two showers," Kurzweil said later. "It was a painstaking effort of trial and error."

By 1973, Kurzweil was ready to make a financial commitment to developing a reading machine. He formed his own company, Kurzweil Computer Products, and scoured the halls at M.I.T. and Harvard to put together a team of experts from a variety of disciplines, including linguistics, phonetics, electrical and mechanical engineering, software design, optics, image processing and education. Money problems plagued the new venture, which was squeezed into a single room in a run-down building in Cambridge; missed paydays and overdue bills were common. But by early 1975, only 18 months after the company's birth, a working model of the Reading Machine was completed. The first commercial model was marketed the following year and was hailed as the greatest advance for the blind since the invention of braille in 1829.

A MUSICAL INSPIRATION

It was an early user of the device, blind rock singer Stevie Wonder, who provided the next challenge for Kurzweil. Hearing of the Reading Machine, Wonder visited Kurzweil and was so impressed by a demonstration that he promptly wrote out a check. Wonder's companions loaded the new machine into the trunk of a taxi, and the singer took it back to his hotel, where he read with it all night long.

Over the next few years, Kurzweil and Wonder kept in touch; the inventor visited Wonder's Los Angeles studio several times, and the singer made several useful suggestions for improving the Reading Machine. In mid-1982, Wonder told Kurzweil that he wanted another kind of machine: an electronic instrument that could accurately mimic the sound of a piano or of any other instrument in an orchestra. Electronic music synthesizers already existed, but Wonder was dissatisfied with them, noting that the sounds they produced were seldom as rich and complex as the sounds made by acoustic instruments. Kurzweil, whose father was a symphony-orchestra conductor, was more than a little interested in music himself; he decided to try to build the device Stevie Wonder sought. But this time, rather than leading the way, he was entering an already crowded field.

By the 1980s, although computerized music was just becoming common, music generated by electricity had a long history. One of the earliest instruments that produced sound by purely electrical means was the Telharmonium, built by American entrepreneur Thaddeus Cahill in the late 1890s. The device sent its electrical music over the rapidly growing telephone network into homes, hotels and restaurants, where it was played through megaphones attached to telephone receivers for "the continuous entertainment of all present." The console for the Telharmonium resembled that of a conventional pipe organ, with two keyboards

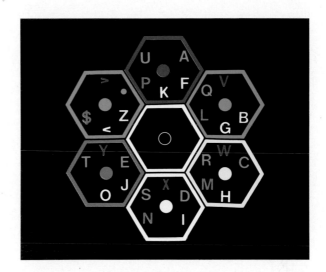

Communicating with the Eyes Alone

The central fact of computer input—that electrical pulses can be turned into digital code—has made it possible to produce machines of astonishing versatility, including a device called the Eyescan Communicator. By translating movements of the eye into signals for a computer, the Eyescan allows people who cannot speak or use keyboards to communicate via computer.

The device, still a prototype, looks deceptively simple. A cylinder the size of a small salt shaker clips onto one lens of a pair of eyeglasses *(below)*. Around its base is a sensor ring containing six infrared light-emitting diodes and six light-sensing cells; within it is a hexagonal display showing the letters of the alphabet and basic punctuation marks. As the user looks at the display, spelling out words by focusing on one letter after another, the sensors pick up the shifting infrared reflections from the surface of the eye. Electrical signals from the sensors travel through a cord either to an ordinary personal computer or to a special microprocessor unit with a small display screen. In either case, a program translates the signals into a message on a display. With access to computer networks, users should be able to write letters, make phone calls, even do their shopping. But the Eyescan's most useful application may be its simplest: "Most people," says inventor Martin King, "just want to be able to say hello."

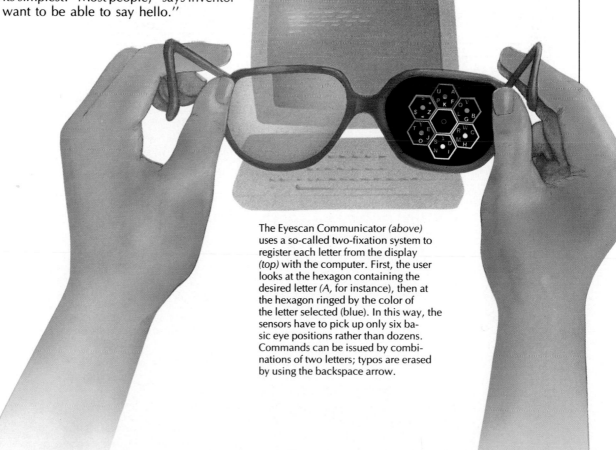

The Eyescan Communicator *(above)* uses a so-called two-fixation system to register each letter from the display *(top)* with the computer. First, the user looks at the hexagon containing the desired letter (A, for instance), then at the hexagon ringed by the color of the letter selected (blue). In this way, the sensors have to pick up only six basic eye positions rather than dozens. Commands can be issued by combinations of two letters; typos are erased by using the backspace arrow.

and a number of stops that could be pulled to vary the timbre. The sound itself came from 35 specially constructed rotary generators large enough to produce the thousands of watts needed to overcome power losses during transmission. In all, the Telharmonium weighed more than 200 tons and required at least a dozen railroad cars to move.

A version of this immensely impractical instrument was installed in Manhattan in 1906, and at first its listeners were amazed. Never before had people heard the pure, perfectly tuned sounds made possible by the mathematical precision of electrical engineering. But before long, the novelty wore off. As one of the musicians who played it noted, "The instrument itself had its own special character, which pervaded everything, and which in time grew highly irritating to the nerves." With the advent of radio, the fate of Cahill's project was sealed.

The concepts behind the Telharmonium lived on, however, surfacing at various times and places over the next several decades. At the Paris Exposition in 1929, for instance, Edouard E. Coupleux and Joseph A. Givelet demonstrated their Automatically Operating Musical Instrument of the Electric Oscillation Type, a four-voice electric music synthesizer controlled by paper tape. The Hammond Organ, which made its public debut in 1935, was basically Cahill's instrument in modern form: The Telharmonium's huge rotary generators were replaced by silver-dollar-size generators whose tones were amplified by vacuum tubes. And in the 1950s, the Radio Corporation of America developed the RCA Synthesizer, which used electronic circuitry to generate and modify sounds.

MAKING MUSIC THE HARD WAY

The RCA Synthesizer superficially resembled computers of the time in that it filled an entire room with its vacuum tubes and wires. However, it was really more like an electronic player piano; its action was controlled by binary codes on wide punched paper tape. Even an advanced version called the Mark II could produce only two tones simultaneously. Complex music was built up by recording one pair of tones on a record-cutting lathe, then setting up another pair of tones and playing back the recording while rerecording the combination on another disk; repeating the cycle produced multilayered music, but the process was lengthy and painstaking. Still, RCA saw great potential for saving money by producing low-cost musical accompaniment for radio and TV programs; there was even speculation that the synthesizer might be used to produce hit records.

The RCA Mark II was an impressive machine, but it was far too expensive and complicated to make electronic music accessible to more than a very few specialists. RCA donated the synthesizer to the Columbia-Princeton Electronic Music Center, founded in 1959, where American composer Milton Babbitt has been one of the few musicians intrepid enough to use it extensively. In the late 1960s, however, electronic music did start to reach a significant audience.

The instrument responsible for this change was invented by a self-employed engineer named Robert Moog (rhymes with "rogue"), then of Trumansburg, New York, and it had a rather piecemeal beginning. Moog at first built voltage-controlled oscillators and amplifiers at the request of a composer friend named Herbert Deutsch. (An oscillator creates a repeating electrical wave whose frequency may be controlled by manipulating the oscillator's voltages.) Eventually, these components evolved into an analog music synthesizer that gave its user control of many simultaneous tones. Moreover, the tones could be rapidly altered, even during a performance. It was a Moog instrument that first produced what the builders of the RCA Mark II had hoped for—a hit record of electronic music. *Switched-On Bach,* an album released in 1968 by a young musician named Walter Carlos, was a totally synthesized interpretation of music by 18th-century composer Johann Sebastian Bach. The album and the instrument that made it possible were together such a breakthrough in electronic music that for years the name of the synthesizer's inventor was a virtual synonym for any synthesizer. Soon composers were writing original music for Moog synthesizers, which began to find wide acceptance in the popular music audience.

THE MATHEMATICAL CONNECTION

While electronic music produced by analog synthesizers was undergoing the development that would end in its being embraced by the pop culture, other experimenters were working out the links between music and digital computers. Western music, with its precise mathematical rules of rhythm and harmony, lends itself easily to digital manipulation. In the late 1950s, as part of his research into voice synthesis, an engineer at Bell Labs named Max Mathews began to investigate the use of computers to generate the sounds of human speech through digital-to-analog converters. Mathews, an amateur violinist, had quickly seen the musical potential of his work, and he encouraged others to explore this field.

In 1960, Mathews and his colleagues created MUSIC, a program that enabled a computer to synthesize musical and other acoustic signals. Shortly thereafter, Bell Labs' first musical work was completed. The piece, which incorporated some primitive synthesized speech, was called *Pitch Variations*. It was not widely performed and got a mostly lukewarm response from audiences; one of Mathews' colleagues later noted that the piece was "cleverly and subtly organized, but the organization didn't come through to the listener."

However, Mathews and Bell engineer John Pierce persevered, composing a few other pieces in a more traditional vein; in 1961, they produced a record called *Music from Mathematics*. Copies were sent to such noted artists as Aaron Copland in an effort, as Pierce put it, "to stir up interest among real composers." Copland's response was polite, but he was not inclined to try the newfangled music himself: "The implications are dizzying and, if I were 20, I would be really concerned at the variety of possibilities suggested," he wrote. "As it is, I plan to be an interested bystander, waiting to see what will happen next."

What happened next was a long campaign to win acceptance. Mathews continued to improve his music-synthesizing software. In 1969, he published MUSIC V, a program that turned a large general-purpose computer such as an IBM System/360 or a PDP-10 into a musical instrument. In essence, composing with the program was done in two parts: The first part spelled out—in mathematical terms—the characteristics of the instruments the computer was to simulate. The second part was, in essence, the musical score—a list of notes to be played by those instruments. As with any other computer program, all of the information was then translated into binary digits, but rather than representing text or data in the more familiar sense, the digits represented frequencies and amplitudes of sound. The computer processed these numbers and produced more numbers, which made up, in effect, a sound file that was stored on magnetic tape and could

The 60-foot-long score of *Love in the Asylum* unrolls from the hands of composer Michael McNabb *(foreground)* and colleagues at Stanford University's Center for Computer Research in Music and Acoustics. The score may be printed out in standard musical notation or in the form shown here, with duration of sound indicated by the length of the lines as measured against a numbered grid.

Hands-Free Help for Astronauts at Work

For astronauts aboard the space shuttle, any repair or maintenance job outside the craft is a considerable challenge. The protective suits necessary to survive in space are cumbersome, and in the absence of gravity, earthly aids such as instruction manuals tend to drift away. A partial solution is to build some of the aids into the spacesuits themselves.

Two of NASA's ideas for experimental spacesuits are shown here and on the following pages. In one version *(below),* a pair of see-through images projected onto the inside of an astronaut's helmet visor provide a view of the project diagram and other data transmitted from a computer aboard the space shuttle. Another possibility *(right)* is to display live images from a video camera; the images could also be viewed simultaneously on earth, where experts can offer guidance as the job progresses. In both versions, a voice-recognition system allows the astronaut to change the display with a spoken command, leaving hands free to do the work.

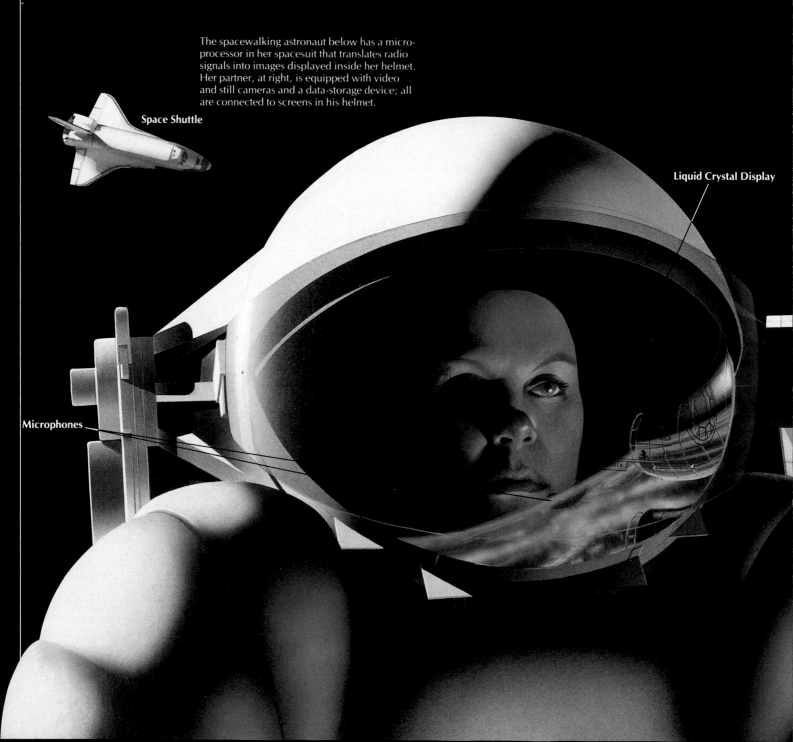

The spacewalking astronaut below has a microprocessor in her spacesuit that translates radio signals into images displayed inside her helmet. Her partner, at right, is equipped with video and still cameras and a data-storage device; all are connected to screens in his helmet.

Space Shuttle

Liquid Crystal Display

Microphones

Still-Image Screen

Video Screen

Video Camera

Data-Storage System

Still Camera

Microphones

Manned
Maneuvering
Unit

An astronaut working in space can check a diagram of the equipment on one visor screen and see a video image of the activity on the other.

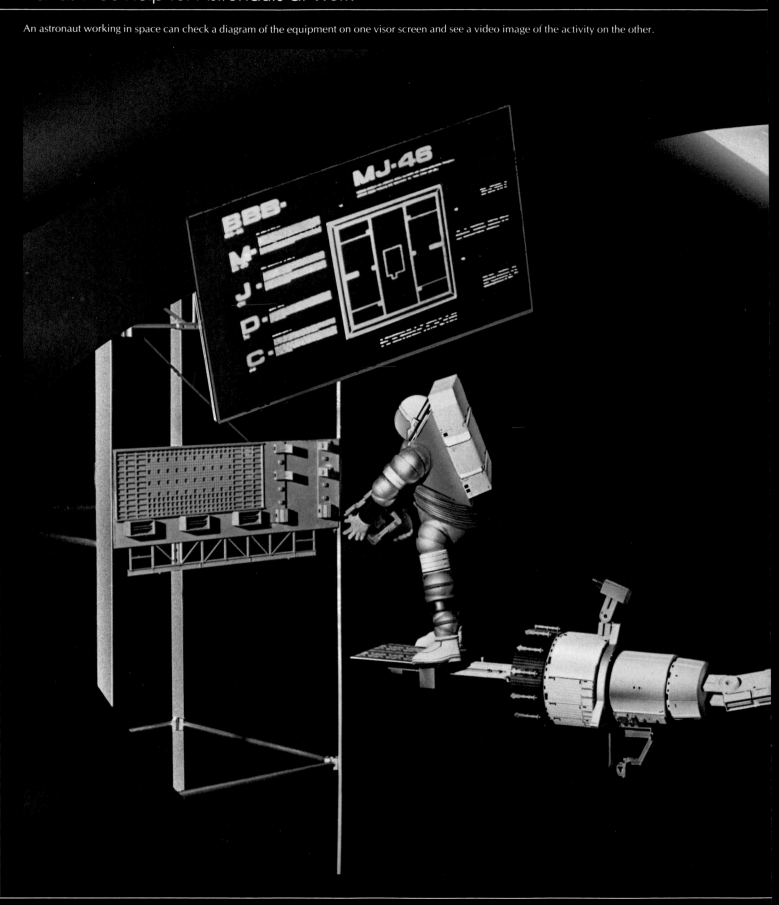

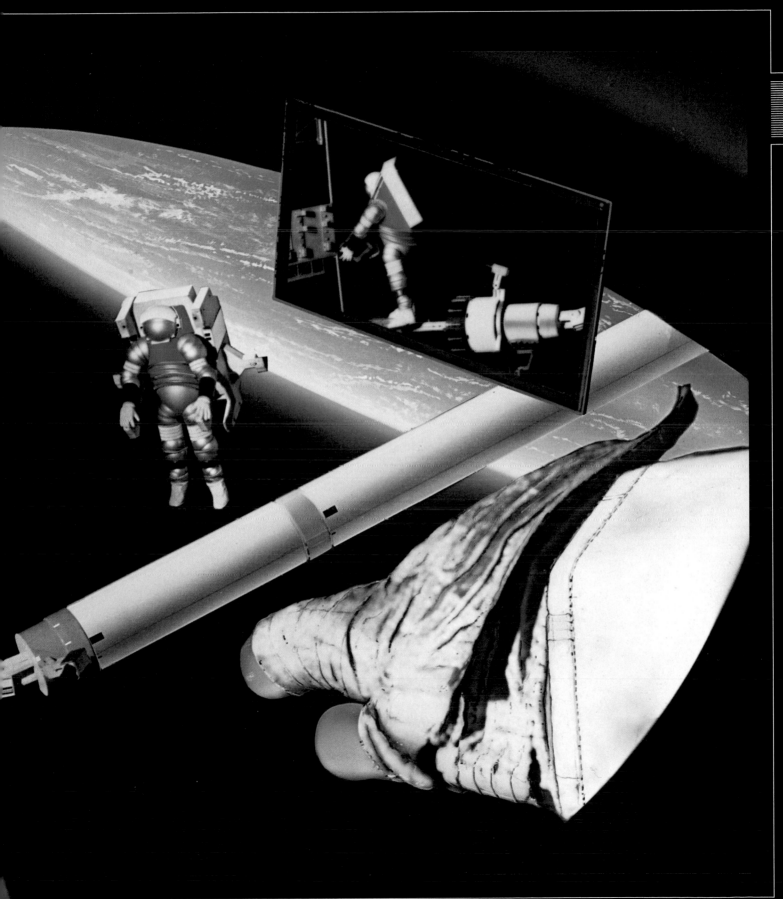

be edited later if desired. When the musician wished to listen to the work, the computer retrieved the file from storage and then passed the binary signals through a digital-to-analog converter that was connected to an amplifier.

The system was powerful but slow; the number crunching required to generate even a second of music was enormous, and a computer musician often had to wait minutes or hours between typing in the numbers of a composition and having a tape ready for conversion into sound.

For all the difficulties presented by early computer-generated music, Mathews' seminal work in the field drew young composers to Bell Labs for periods of study in the 1960s. Because his programs did not rely on the input of sound generated by analog devices, computer musicians were utterly free to invent and experiment. One who came to Bell Labs early on was a Stanford University music-composition student named John Chowning, who had read Mathews' first papers on computer music and went east for a brief time to learn his methods.

A SHORTCUT TO COMPLEX SYNTHESIS

Upon returning to California, Chowning began haunting Stanford's artificial-intelligence laboratory to cadge time on the lab's computer. For several years, he labored at the crossroads of music and computers. Then, in 1973, he published a paper that would have a far-reaching effect on computer music. Chowning's theory of digital frequency modulation, or digital FM *(pages 118-119)*, led to a programming technique that enabled computer musicians to achieve rich, complex synthesized sounds without lengthy computer processing. Suddenly, the live performance of computer-generated music, which had always been frustratingly out of reach, seemed possible. In 1975, Chowning founded the Center for Computer Research in Music and Acoustics (CCRMA, pronounced "karma"), which soon became a hotbed of composition and performance. Similar centers sprang up around the country and in Europe, attracting young musicians who appreciated the creative control that computers offered. As one CCRMA composer said, "We can put these sounds into space, move them around, add reverberation, make a singer in a small room sound as if he's singing in a huge cathedral."

In Paris, Pierre Boulez, a renowned composer and conductor, founded IRCAM (Institute for Research and Coordination of Acoustics and Music) in 1977. Over the next few years, Boulez worked on a piece entitled *Répons (Response)*. First performed in 1981, it was scored for three groups to play simultaneously. An instrumental ensemble of 24 musicians sat on a raised platform in the center, facing the conductor. Stationed around the room were several soloists, also on platforms, whose instruments (electric organ, harp, cimbalom, vibraphone, xylophone and two pianos) were connected by cables to a central bank of electronic equipment. Situated behind the conductor and operated by half a dozen technicians, this system had at its center a computer, the 4X, developed at IRCAM. The 4X Music Workstation, as the system was called, made use of several techniques of sound synthesis, including digital FM; it could thus alter sounds fed into it from the live soloists fast enough to allow it to function as an instrument itself. *Répons* was favorably reviewed (one critic likened the complexity of the 18-minute concert to "the turning of a gigantic wheel in space"), and Boulez continued to develop the piece, more than doubling its length over the next few years.

Répons was proof that computer music was ready to come out of the laborato-

Inventor Raymond Kurzweil shows off the Kurzweil 250, a computerized keyboard designed to reproduce the rich sounds of piano, guitar, trumpet and at least 27 other instruments. His secret: a memory bank in which the complex tones produced by each instrument are recorded in the form of mathematical models.

ry. The large mainframes needed by early workers such as Chowning at CCRMA and Mathews at Bell Labs had made the systems impractical for stage performance. But the advent of integrated circuits and inexpensive computer memory brought drastic reductions in the size and price of computer-music synthesizers. Yamaha, a Japanese manufacturer of analog electronic synthesizers similar to the Moog, recognized the potential of digital FM and obtained a license to use CCRMA's patents. By 1980, the company had developed a piano-size digital FM keyboard that could be programmed with a number of different voices, all provided by the manufacturer on magnetic cards. And then the floodgates opened. Raymond Kurzweil, spurred by Stevie Wonder's request, founded a new company that by 1983 had produced a prototype portable piano synthesizer so sophisticated that many listeners—even professional musicians—were hard pressed to distinguish it from a concert grand piano. Yamaha continued to miniaturize its synthesizers, developing portable keyboards that were smaller, more versatile and much less expensive than its own first model.

With increased memory and programming capacity, sophisticated digital music synthesizers were becoming, in effect, specialized computers. When music-composition and -performance software began to appear for general-purpose microcomputers, the issue of compatibility arose. In August 1983, leading manufacturers of synthesizers reached an agreement on a software and hardware standard for sending digital data between electronic instruments. MIDI, as the agreement is called (for Musical Instrument Digital Interface), allows computer musicians to link several synthesizers with one another, as well as with a computer, through an extra socket, called a MIDI port. This was basically the same as the plug ports used to hook up computers and ordinary I/O devices such as printers.

A PLUG-COMPATIBLE ORCHESTRA

The new plug compatibility among synthesizers and between synthesizers and computers was a breakthrough akin to that made by IBM's System/360 two decades earlier. Now, by using one synthesizer as the master keyboard and programming the others with the voices of various instruments, a musician could become a one-person orchestra. With different programming, the same musician could produce, in live performance, the kind of complex layering of sound once possible only in a recording studio. And anyone with a MIDI-equipped computer could enter notes at a keyboard (either a synthesizer's or the computer's, depending on the software), store them on disk or tape, and then edit them and play them back through one or more synthesizers. Robert Moog, for one, discerns in the marriage of computers and music the potential for a profound change: "I think we're on the threshold of seeing computer-based home music systems replacing the piano as something that young children learn music on."

Unlike Western music, with its mathematical precision, other, more free-form arts, took to computers slowly. In the visual arts, some avant-garde creators began to adapt the techniques for computerized image making that had become standard tools in television and film production during the 1970s. Critical acceptance of the new medium was grudging, but the introduction in the 1980s of personal computers equipped with graphics-input devices spread the technology widely, and computer art was transformed from curiosity to commonplace.

Computers have also begun to find their place in the field of dance, which has

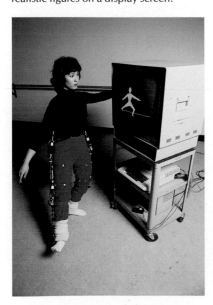

Wrapped in sensors called goniometers, which measure a joint's angle and range of movement, a dancer imitates the stance of a computer-generated image. The goniometers, designed to transmit leg movements directly to the computer, are part of an experimental teaching device that may one day be able to record entire dances and play them back with realistic figures on a display screen.

An Artistic Mélange

Perhaps no form of computer output is viewed with more skepticism than computer art; critics have debated its merits for more than 20 years. But to many artists—including the four whose work is shown here—the computer is simply another tool. David Em, for example, relishes the power to control every dot of an image *(below)*. The animators at Lucasfilm strive for photorealism *(far right, top)*, while Keith Haring, known for his graffiti art, simply enjoys the challenge of creating his work in a new medium *(far right, bottom)*. Harold Cohen, who produces sketches with a machine programmed with arbitrary rules for drawing lines, is less interested in the machine's final product *(right)* than in how those who see the machine in action credit it with artistic intention.

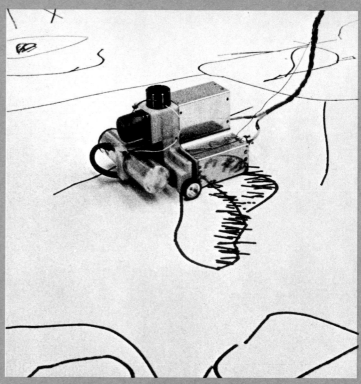

Guided by artist Harold Cohen's computer, a so-called turtle, a rolling instrument equipped with a pen *(right)*, creates a childlike drawing.

David Em's *Gabriel (below)*, produced using four integrated graphics programs, is one frame from an animated film.

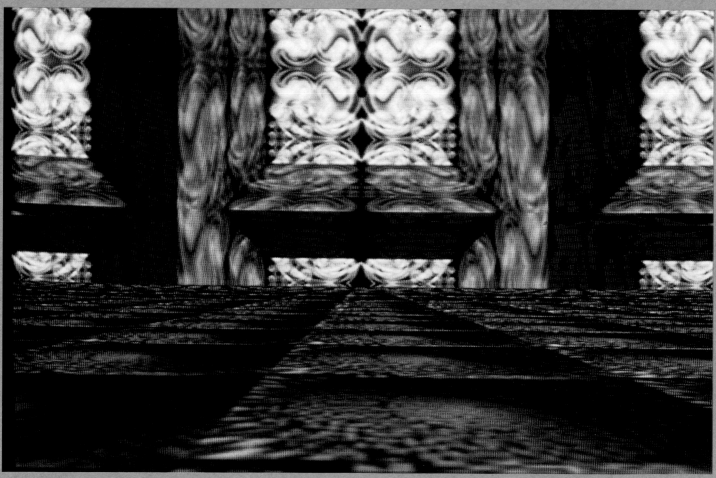

A frame from the Lucasfilm cartoon *The Adventures of André and Wally B.* *(above)* reveals the realistic detail possible when 10 programmers have access to 10 powerful minicomputers and two Cray supercomputers.

Keith Haring created this computer image *(right)* during a visit to Tokyo in 1982. The image was then photographed from the computer's screen.

sometimes been characterized as the illiterate art. Although a number of notation systems make it possible to create a written record of an existing dance, the systems are difficult to master and time-consuming to execute. Skilled notators are scarce, and they must usually see a piece performed at least four times to catch all of its movements. As a result, it may require weeks to take down, by hand, the steps of even a short ballet. Not surprisingly, a written archive of the world's dance repertoire is almost nonexistent. Furthermore, none of the notation systems produce a score that performers can follow in the way musicians can follow a musical score; every dance must be taught by demonstration.

Since the early 1970s, choreographers and computer scientists have worked together to develop systems that can preserve the fundamental steps and movements of a dance. One of the earliest experimenters was Thomas Calvert, a biomedical engineer at Simon Fraser University in British Columbia. Calvert, who was specializing in the study of motion, brought together computer graphics and Labanotation, the most common symbolic representation of dance.

Calvert's first programs set up a model on the screen called Stick Figure, which could respond with realistic speed to modified Labanotation commands entered through the keyboard. But Stick Figure's lack of dimension on the screen often made it hard to tell what direction the figure was facing, or whether the figure was turning clockwise or counterclockwise. As more powerful computers began to expand the capacity of animation during the early 1980s, however, Calvert managed to create the illusion of depth by making the lines at the edge of a more fleshed-out figure disappear as the figure turns away from the viewer; the lines reappear as the figure turns forward. The model's position can be changed by typing in simple instructions such as EXTEND FOREARM; more complex actions are called up with extended sets of commands. The computer's translation of a Labanotation score sometimes results in jerky movement on the screen, a problem Calvert addressed by programming more than 50 English-language commands to help smooth out such actions as walking, hopping and jumping.

Calvert next began working on a system for entering movement into the computer without the keyboard. The method employs goniometers attached to a dancer's joints. These angle-measuring devices, similar to the sensors that helped Nan Davis maintain her balance, transmit electrical signals through an analog-to-digital converter directly to the computer, which instructs the screen figure to replicate the dancer's stance. Systems such as this can be used to generate a complete score, which may take either written (Labanotation) or animated form, directly from a dancer's movements. Such systems can assume some of the choreographer's teaching role as well. When a dance is stored electronically, dancers can use the computer to learn the basic movements of a piece, leaving the choreographer free to concentrate on the dancers' interpretations.

The work of researchers such as Thomas Calvert in dance or Max Mathews and John Chowning in music exemplifies the powerful influence that computers with innovative systems for input and output can have on society. Music synthesis already has changed not only the sounds broadcast over popular radio but the very way musicians think about creating and recording their compositions. Similarly, the ability to compile a true library of dance will have a lasting effect on that discipline, allowing a work to be more easily passed on from company to company and generation to generation.

A New Definition of Control in Music and Sound

5

Music is the art of giving a pleasing pattern to sounds generated by the human voice or mechanical means—the vibration of a reed or string or drumhead, for example. As a rule, composers take the sounds produced by voices or instruments as givens, shaping them with rhythm and melody, determining how loudly or softly a note should be played. The sounds themselves—their tonal qualities, that is—are governed by the physical properties of the instruments that produce them.

Now composers and performers can choose something very different: the computer. As a means of musical expression, it is in a class by itself; unlike all other instruments, the computer has no unique voice of its own. Without auxiliary analog equipment to convert its digital output into something audible, the machine is mute. Yet given the right input, it can generate sound waves that mimic almost any voice, with a fidelity that can make the synthetic virtually indistinguishable from the natural. More important, it offers a degree of artistic freedom and control utterly new in music. With the computer's aid, musicians can create, store and replay sounds in innumerable combinations. Computer musicians are even developing software for generating mathematical models of instruments unlike any known in the physical world.

Modern as it may seem, the idea of using computers to make music traces back to Augusta Ada Byron, the Countess of Lovelace, whose work on the never completed Analytical Engine in the 1840s *(page 8)* foreshadowed much of modern programming. Observing the mathematical nature of the relationship of musical sounds—for example, a note in one octave is exactly twice as high as the corresponding note an octave lower—Lovelace suggested that the engine "might compose elaborate and scientific pieces of music of any degree of complexity." As the following pages demonstrate, Lovelace was about 120 years ahead of her time.

Revealing the Intricate Structure of Sound

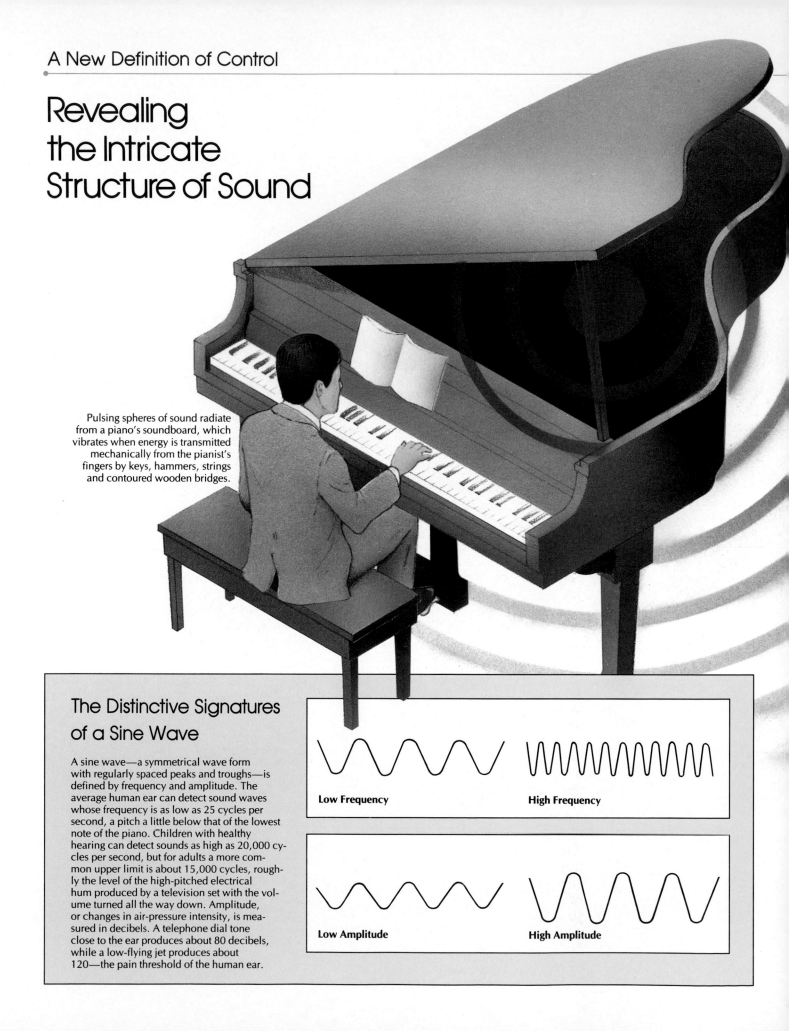

Pulsing spheres of sound radiate from a piano's soundboard, which vibrates when energy is transmitted mechanically from the pianist's fingers by keys, hammers, strings and contoured wooden bridges.

The Distinctive Signatures of a Sine Wave

A sine wave—a symmetrical wave form with regularly spaced peaks and troughs—is defined by frequency and amplitude. The average human ear can detect sound waves whose frequency is as low as 25 cycles per second, a pitch a little below that of the lowest note of the piano. Children with healthy hearing can detect sounds as high as 20,000 cycles per second, but for adults a more common upper limit is about 15,000 cycles, roughly the level of the high-pitched electrical hum produced by a television set with the volume turned all the way down. Amplitude, or changes in air-pressure intensity, is measured in decibels. A telephone dial tone close to the ear produces about 80 decibels, while a low-flying jet produces about 120—the pain threshold of the human ear.

Low Frequency

High Frequency

Low Amplitude

High Amplitude

All musical sounds, or tones, are simply changes in air pressure; so are all noises. But with noise, the changes are random, while with tones they are repeated in a discernible pattern that lends itself to musical organization. A vibrating tuning fork, for instance, pushes air molecules back and forth, causing the air pressure around it to increase and decrease repeatedly. This pattern of changes forms a spherically spreading pressure wave that the human ear perceives as sound.

Pressure waves may be graphed mathematically as wave forms, the simplest of which is called a sine wave *(box, below, left)*. Sine waves are defined by two properties, frequency and amplitude. Frequency is the number of times per second that a wave cycle (one peak and one trough) repeats; the brain interprets this as pitch, the highness or lowness of the sound. Amplitude—the intensity of the change in air pressure—is translated by ear and brain into loudness. Like all repeating waves, the pressure waves that form musical sounds are made up of scores of sine waves of varying frequencies. In 1822, Jean Baptiste Fourier, the French mathematician and physicist who discovered the complex structure of repeating waves, published a powerful mathematical technique for reducing such waves to their component sine waves. Fourier analysis, as the technique is known, can now be incorporated into programs that enable computers to perform the kind of analysis accomplished automatically by the discriminating human ear.

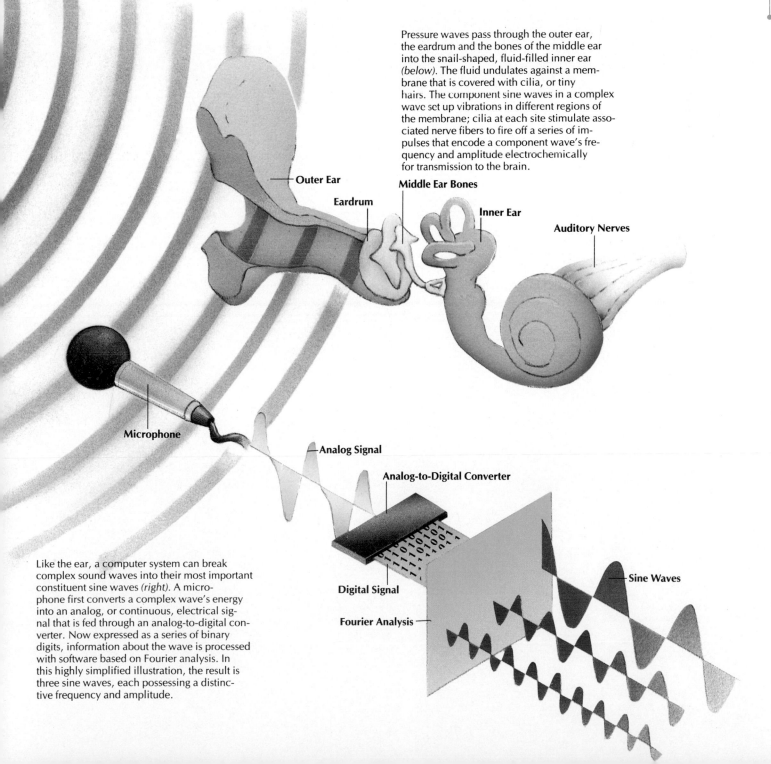

Pressure waves pass through the outer ear, the eardrum and the bones of the middle ear into the snail-shaped, fluid-filled inner ear *(below)*. The fluid undulates against a membrane that is covered with cilia, or tiny hairs. The component sine waves in a complex wave set up vibrations in different regions of the membrane; cilia at each site stimulate associated nerve fibers to fire off a series of impulses that encode a component wave's frequency and amplitude electrochemically for transmission to the brain.

Outer Ear

Eardrum

Middle Ear Bones

Inner Ear

Auditory Nerves

Microphone

Analog Signal

Analog-to-Digital Converter

Digital Signal

Fourier Analysis

Sine Waves

Like the ear, a computer system can break complex sound waves into their most important constituent sine waves *(right)*. A microphone first converts a complex wave's energy into an analog, or continuous, electrical signal that is fed through an analog-to-digital converter. Now expressed as a series of binary digits, information about the wave is processed with software based on Fourier analysis. In this highly simplified illustration, the result is three sine waves, each possessing a distinctive frequency and amplitude.

Building Sound through Addition

If a complex sound can be reduced to its component waves by Fourier analysis, it can also be built up using a similar method. One technique employed by computer musicians is called additive synthesis; in this process, software generates digital descriptions of individual sine waves and combines them mathematically to form a complex wave *(below)*.

The particular combination of sine waves that make up a given complex wave determines a note's timbre—that is, whether it sounds like a trumpet or a piano. For any sound, the lowest-frequency sine wave, which is often also the loudest, is called the fundamental; it determines the pitch of the com-

In this simplified example, an additive synthesis program generates five sine waves mathematically—a low-frequency fundamental wave and four higher-frequency overtones—then combines them. Simultaneous peaks reinforce one another, as do simultaneous troughs; peaks and troughs occurring at the same time offset one another. The resulting wave has a complex profile: a pitch dictated by the fundamental, with richness added by the overtones.

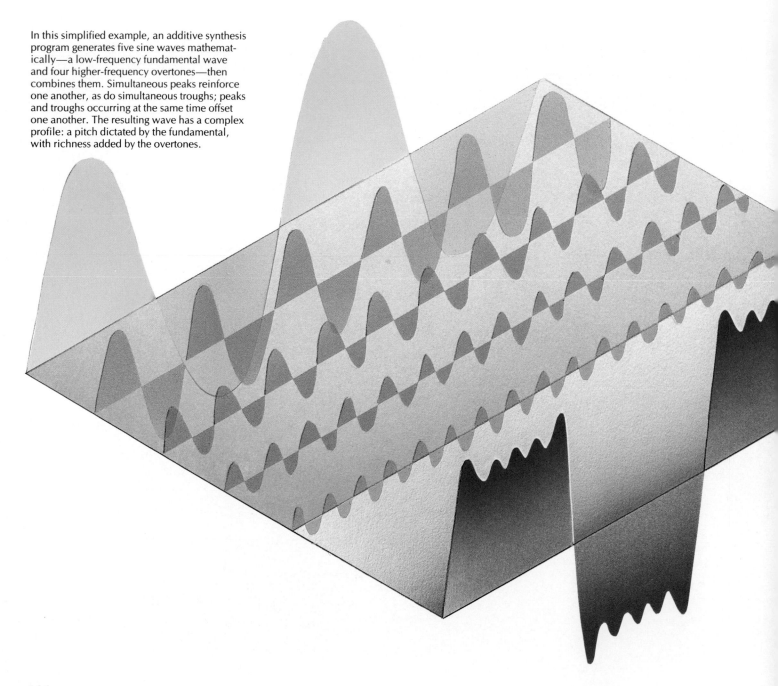

plex wave. Higher frequencies, which are usually quieter, are called overtones. Another factor in defining an entire note's tonal quality is the envelope, or characteristic amplitude and frequency pattern, of a note played by a given instrument *(below, right)*. The pattern includes three phases: the attack, as the note builds from silence to its full volume; the sustain, when it remains more or less at full volume; and the decay, when it dies away. The number of calculations needed to produce a single note of one second's duration is many tens of thousands—making this method an example of the brute-force approach to music synthesis.

Notes produced by three different instruments—cello, trumpet and bass drum—have characteristically different envelopes, or frequency and amplitude patterns *(right)*. The cello's attack phase, as it builds volume, is gradual compared with the trumpet's abrupt attack. For both cello and trumpet, the sustain period is relatively long, in contrast to the bass drum's fleeting sustain phase, which is followed by a lengthy and erratic decay.

Cello

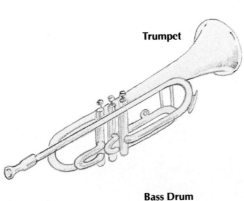

Trumpet

Bass Drum

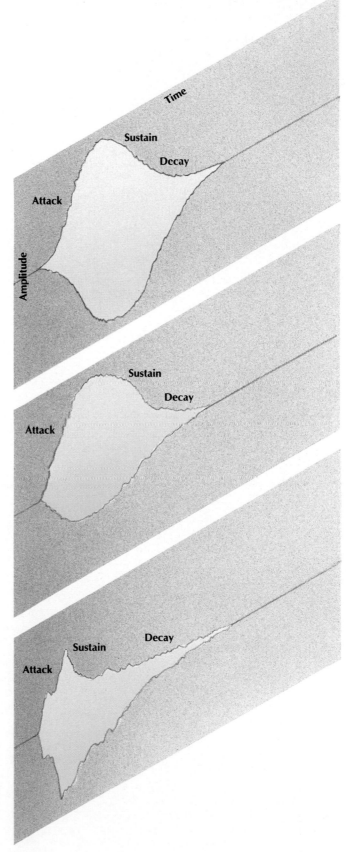

Sculpting Sound through Subtraction

Addition of sine waves is one approach to sound synthesis, subtraction another. The computer composer who makes music by subtractive synthesis works like a sculptor, chiseling away unwanted frequencies from a noisy signal made up of a mixture of frequencies.

One model for subtractive synthesis is the process by which the human vocal instrument produces song. Air forced out of the lungs picks up a rich mixture of frequencies when it encounters the vibrating vocal cords. As the airstream continues through the vocal tract—the passage stretching from the vocal cords to the lips—some of the frequencies

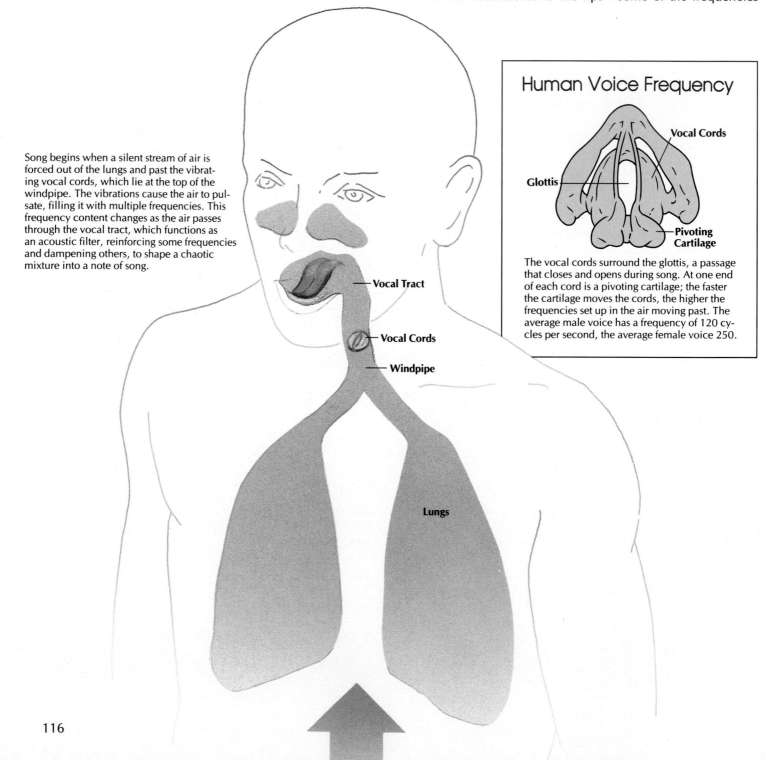

Song begins when a silent stream of air is forced out of the lungs and past the vibrating vocal cords, which lie at the top of the windpipe. The vibrations cause the air to pulsate, filling it with multiple frequencies. This frequency content changes as the air passes through the vocal tract, which functions as an acoustic filter, reinforcing some frequencies and dampening others, to shape a chaotic mixture into a note of song.

Vocal Tract

Vocal Cords

Windpipe

Lungs

Human Voice Frequency

Vocal Cords

Glottis

Pivoting Cartilage

The vocal cords surround the glottis, a passage that closes and opens during song. At one end of each cord is a pivoting cartilage; the faster the cartilage moves the cords, the higher the frequencies set up in the air moving past. The average male voice has a frequency of 120 cycles per second, the average female voice 250.

are reinforced, resonating against the walls of that passage and becoming louder. Others are weakened to the point that they may be completely inaudible by the time they pass through the lips. The shifting positions of the tongue, movements of the jaw, and changes in the size and shape of the opening between the lips give the vocal tract a constantly changing pattern of resonances.

To synthesize song, the computer generates a series of numbers representing a complex pulselike signal; like the sound produced by the vocal cords, the signal is loaded with varying frequencies. The signal becomes input for a program

that can be derived from a type of analysis of the human voice known as linear prediction. In effect, the program acts as a filter, emphasizing the strongest frequencies of the desired voice. It is thus possible to synthesize a soprano voice, for example, by programming the filter to emphasize frequencies around 3,000 cycles per second, the so-called singing formant of a typical human soprano.

The output of the filter—a note of a song—is in numerical form. For performance, the sequence of numbers coding the song is processed by a digital-to-analog converter, which generates a corresponding sequence of discrete pulses of voltage. A so-called low-pass filter smoothes the individual pulses into a continuous signal, which a loudspeaker transforms into audible pressure waves.

The signal then passes through a mathematical filter that can be based on analysis of human song to determine the combination of frequencies that will yield a natural-sounding tone. Those frequencies are reinforced; other frequencies are diminished.

In the first step of subtractive synthesis of the human voice, the computer generates a complex, pulselike signal containing numerous sine waves at harmonically related frequencies. (This signal, which will produce vowel sounds, may be combined with another one that is similar to so-called white, or random, noise, which replicates the consonants in human speech.)

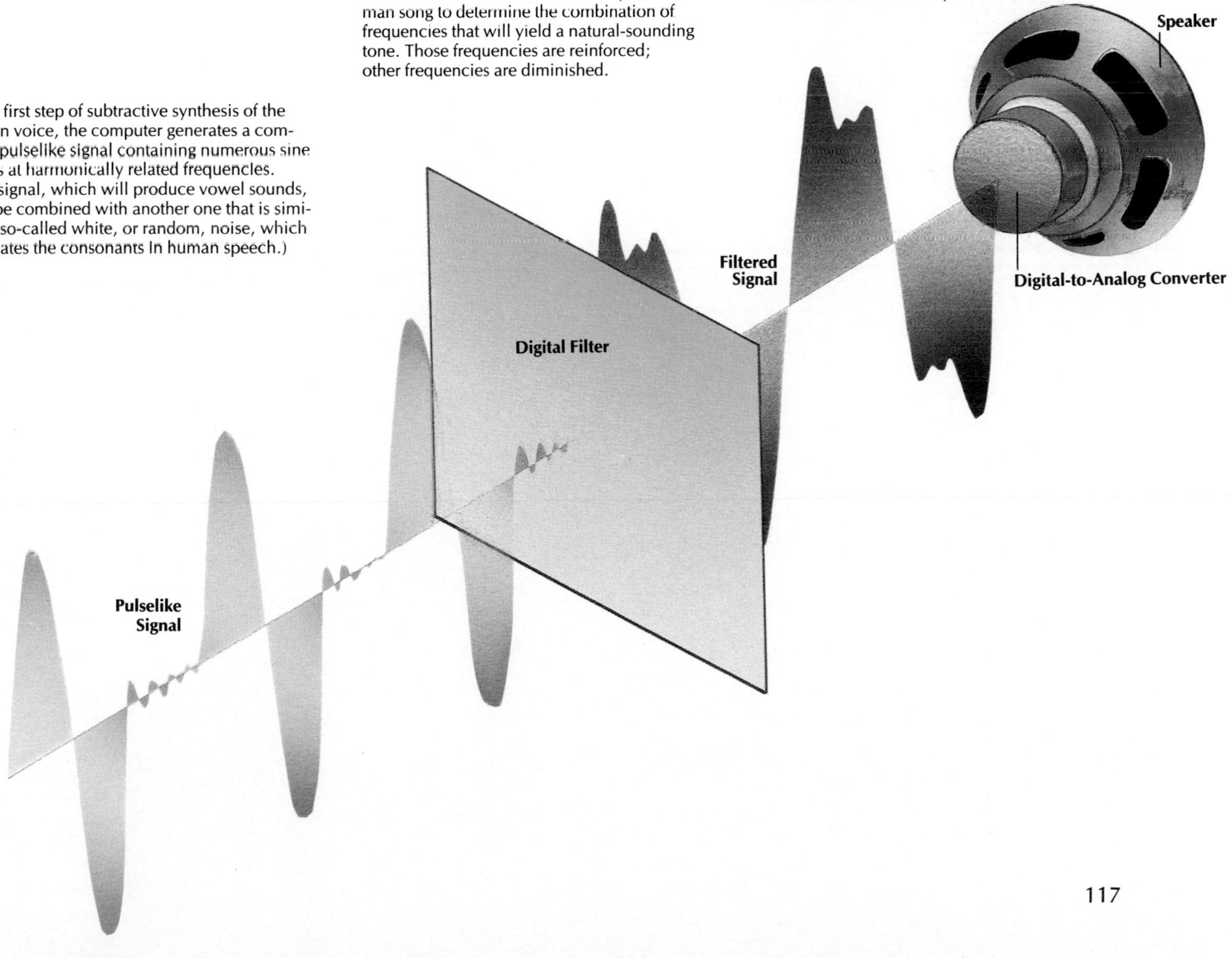

Speaker

Filtered Signal

Digital-to-Analog Converter

Digital Filter

Pulselike Signal

Efficient Synthesis by Multiplication

A technique called digital FM (frequency modulation) gives sounds tonal richness without huge computational effort. Unlike the FM used in radio broadcasting, which involves analog electrical signals, digital FM is purely a mathematical exercise. Program subroutines called FM oscillators generate sine waves of different frequencies. Depending on the order in which the oscillators are employed, the waves may be either modulators, which modify other waves, or carriers, which are the waves acted upon by modulators.

In a process akin to multiplication, a modulator wave is fed through an oscillator acting as a carrier, to produce a complex modulated wave *(below)*. This modulated wave has the frequency generated by the carrier, with multiple overtones supplied by the modulator; the modulated wave may even possess some of the random noise present in the sounds produced on conventional instruments. Tens of thousands of calculations are required for every second of sound, but since only a few waves are manipulated, rather than the dozens involved in additive synthesis, the process calls for far less computer power.

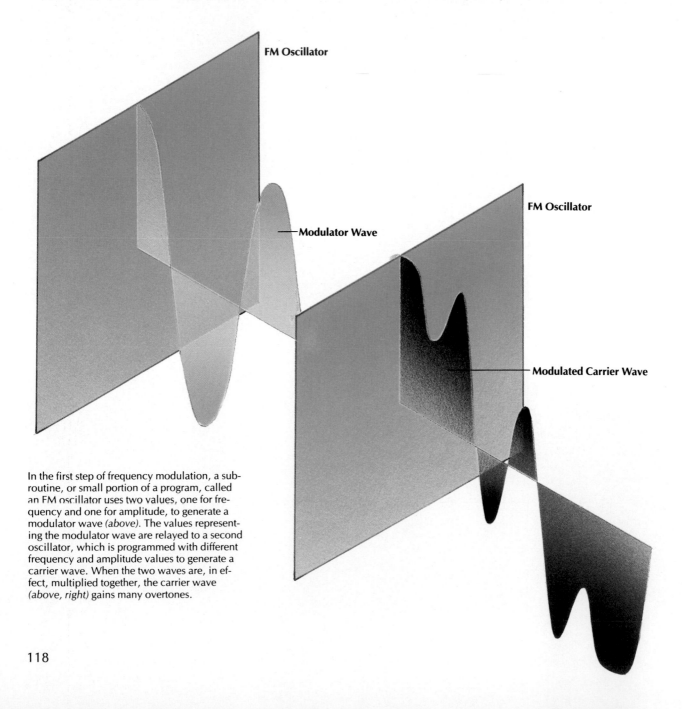

FM Oscillator

Modulator Wave

FM Oscillator

Modulated Carrier Wave

In the first step of frequency modulation, a subroutine, or small portion of a program, called an FM oscillator uses two values, one for frequency and one for amplitude, to generate a modulator wave *(above)*. The values representing the modulator wave are relayed to a second oscillator, which is programmed with different frequency and amplitude values to generate a carrier wave. When the two waves are, in effect, multiplied together, the carrier wave *(above, right)* gains many overtones.

An Algorithmic Keyboard

The keyboard of a digital FM synthesizer may look like that of a piano, but the resemblance is only superficial. Instead of creating sound by transmitting finger pressure to hammers, strings and soundboard, the synthesizer's keys trigger electronic impulses that call up FM oscillators. Oscillators may be linked according to recipes called algorithms to generate different voices. The synthesizer can store these algorithms, along with characteristics the composer can use during a performance, such as vibrato, volume or purposeful distortion.

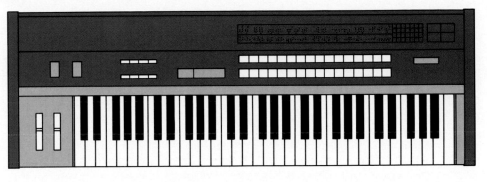

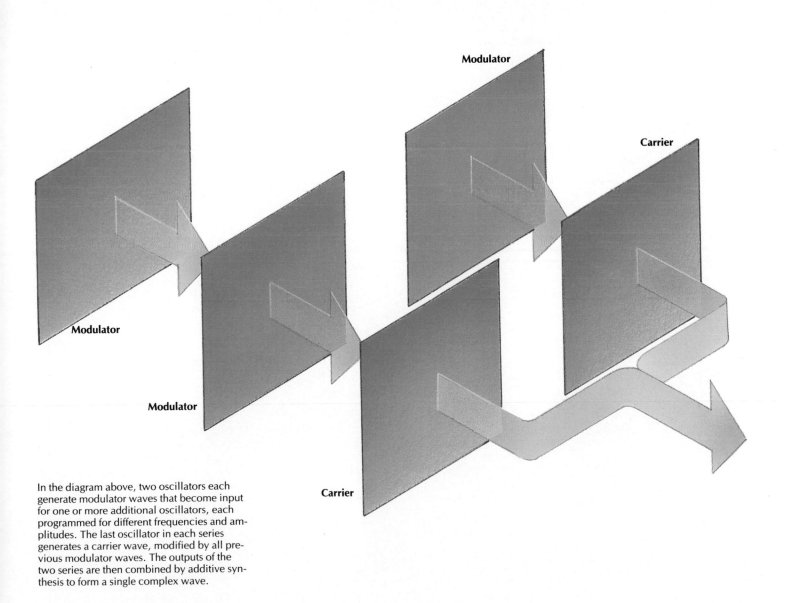

Modulator

Carrier

Modulator

Modulator

Carrier

In the diagram above, two oscillators each generate modulator waves that become input for one or more additional oscillators, each programmed for different frequencies and amplitudes. The last oscillator in each series generates a carrier wave, modified by all previous modulator waves. The outputs of the two series are then combined by additive synthesis to form a single complex wave.

Creating Instruments of the Imagination

In the techniques of frequency modulation as well as both additive and subtractive synthesis, the process of creating sound with a computer is based on an analysis of real sound waves. A fourth, and more radical, method begins at an earlier stage in the chronology of sound, with the physics of an instrument—but the instrument need not be real.

A mathematical model that incorporates some or all of the physical characteristics of the instrument is employed to generate the wave forms that arise from those characteristics. One

To create a mathematical model of a violin string, the programmer must prescribe the string's length, stiffness and tension. The model must also account for the dampening effect the supports at each end of the string have on the string's vibration. The mathematically defined friction of the bow against the string, its distance from the end supports, and its velocity and pressure all affect the sound wave generated by the model.

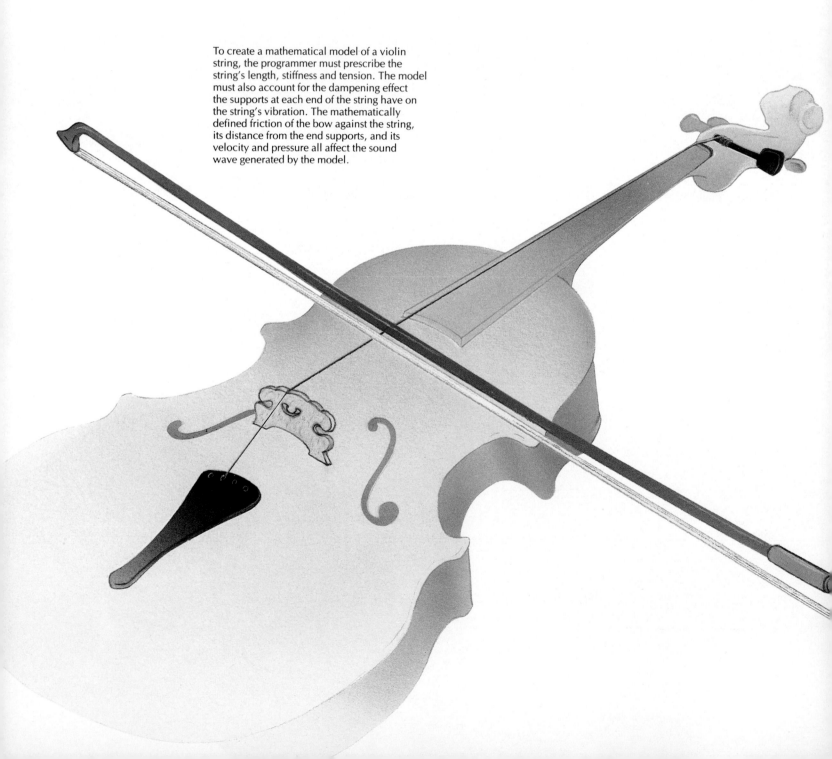

such model, for example, can simulate the physical characteristics of a vibrating violin string and a bow, as well as the ways in which they interact. Input for the model includes variables that affect frequency and amplitude, such as string length, the speed with which the bow moves across the string and the changing pressure the bow exerts on the string. To make the final sound richer and less harsh, the model would also have to include a mathematical description of the wooden body of a real violin.

But there is no reason to limit this modeling method to violins or any other real-world instrument. The process frees composers to create instruments to suit their fancies or their musical needs; the computer allows them to ignore the limitations of physical reality.

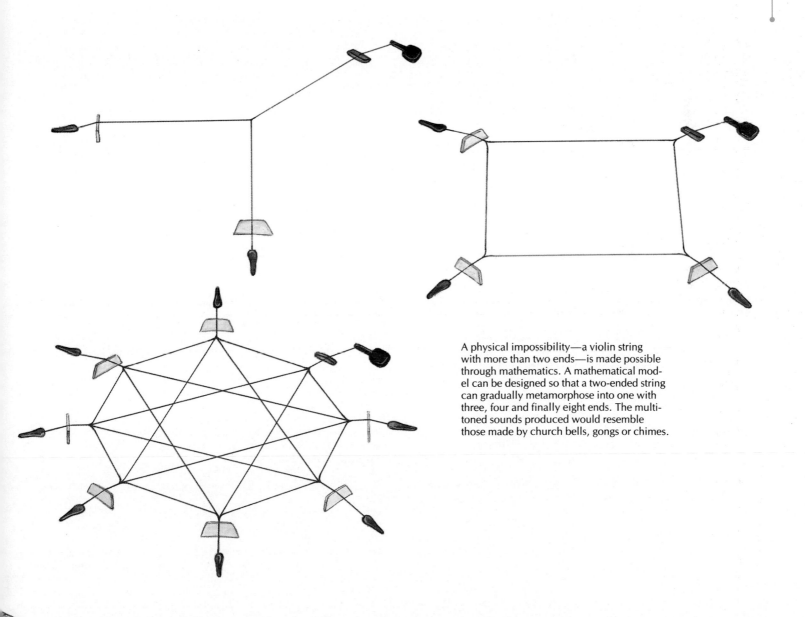

A physical impossibility—a violin string with more than two ends—is made possible through mathematics. A mathematical model can be designed so that a two-ended string can gradually metamorphose into one with three, four and finally eight ends. The multitoned sounds produced would resemble those made by church bells, gongs or chimes.

Glossary

American Standard Code for Information Interchange (ASCII): a convention that assigns a standard binary code to each upper- and lower-case character, numeral and typographical symbol.

Analog: the representation of a continuously changing physical variable (sound, for example) by another physical variable (such as electrical current).

Analog computer: a computer in which continuous physical variables such as the movement of gears or the magnitude of voltage represent data.

Analog-to-digital converter: a device that changes an analog signal into digital information.

Bar code: a machine-readable code consisting of ink lines that represent information such as a product description and price.

Binary: having two components or possible states; usually represented by a code of zeros and ones.

Bit: the smallest unit of information in a binary computer, represented by a single zero or one. The word "bit" is a contraction of "binary digit."

Bit map: a temporary memory for a graphic display in which each dot, or pixel, of the display is represented by one or more bits.

Buffer: a temporary memory used to hold data being transferred from one device to another, such as from a computer to a printer.

Bus: a conductor or set of conductors that transmits information between parts of a computer.

Byte: a sequence of bits, usually eight, treated as a unit for computation or storage.

Cathode-ray tube (CRT): a television-like display device with a screen that lights up where it is struck from the inside by a beam of electrons.

Central processing unit (CPU): the part of a computer that interprets and executes instructions. It is composed of an arithmetic logic unit, a control unit and a small amount of memory.

Chip: *see* integrated circuit.

Computer-aided design (CAD): the use of a computer to create or modify a design.

Computer-aided manufacture (CAM): the use of a computer in the manufacturing of a product.

Cursor: a moving spot of light that indicates a point of action or attention on a computer screen.

Daisy-wheel printer: a printer with a circular print element consisting of thin stems, with characters on their ends, radiating out from a central hub.

Digital: pertaining to the representation, manipulation or transmission of information by discrete, or on-off, signals.

Digital computer: a machine that operates on data expressed in discrete form rather than the continuous representation used in an analog computer.

Digitize: to convert analog information into binary-coded on-off signals that can represent the information within a digital computer.

Digitizing tablet: a device that allows the user to enter drawings into the computer as a sequence of coordinates by moving a hand-held control over a flat tablet.

Direct memory access (DMA): a mechanism that transmits data directly between a computer's input/output ports and its temporary memory.

Disk: a round magnetized plate, generally made of plastic or metal, used for storing data.

Dot-matrix printer: an impact printer that uses a pattern of dots arranged in rows and columns to print text or graphics.

Electrostatic printer: a nonimpact printer that employs particles of dry ink, which cling in the desired pattern to electrically charged paper. Also called a laser printer.

Fiber optics: the technology of encoding data as pulses of laser light beamed through ultrathin strands of glass.

Goniometer: an instrument that measures angles; in computer-aided choreography, electronic goniometers communicate information about the range of movement in a dancer's joints.

Hacker: an avid experimenter with computers.

Hard copy: printed computer output, usually on paper.

Icon: a symbol that represents a command or an object on a display screen.

Impact printer: a printer that works by striking a raised character or a pin against paper through an inked ribbon.

Ink-jet printer: a nonimpact printer that works by spraying electrically charged droplets of ink onto paper.

Input: information fed into a computer.

Integrated circuit: an electronic circuit whose components are formed on a single piece of semiconductor material (a substance, such as silicon, whose conductivity falls between that of a metal and an insulator).

Interface: electronic circuitry that allows two devices to communicate with each other.

Interrupt: a temporary halt in executing a program, or the signal that causes that halt.

Joystick: a hand-held lever that can be tilted in various directions to control the movement of a cursor on a display screen.

Keyboard: an arrangement of keys, like those on a typewriter, used to enter data into a computer.

Laser printer: *see* electrostatic printer.

Light-emitting diode (LED): a semiconductor device that emits light when a current passes through it.

Light pen: a pen-shaped photosensitive input device used to direct the computer or to draw images by touching a CRT display.

Liquid crystal display (LCD): a digital display device made up of character-forming segments of liquid crystal material sandwiched between polarizing and reflecting pieces of glass.

Look-up table: an area of memory set aside for a table of values that is referred to when necessary for a program.

Magnetic tape: plastic tape coated with a magnetic material on which information is stored in the form of magnetized spots.

Menu: a list of commands, functions or graphic symbols shown on a display screen or a digitizing tablet.

Microchip: *see* integrated circuit.

Microprocessor: a single chip containing all the elements of a computer's central processing unit.

Modem: a device (modulator/demodulator) that enables data to be transmitted between computers, generally over telephone lines but sometimes on fiber-optic cable or radio frequencies.

Monitor: a television-like device for displaying data.

Mouse: a hand-held input device that, when rolled across a flat surface, causes a cursor to move in a corresponding way on a display screen.

On-line: immediately accessible by a computer's CPU. Refers to the technique of entering data and instructions directly into a computer.

Optical character reader (OCR): a unit capable of recognizing characters in a special typeface, such as those on a bank check.

Oscilloscope: an output device that displays a signal in wave form on a CRT.

Output: the data presented by a computer either directly to the user, to another computer or to some form of storage.

Paper tape: a continuous strip of paper about one inch wide on which data is recorded in the form of punched holes; used either for input or for output.

Paper-tape reader: a device used to enter data from a punched paper tape into a computer by translating the pattern of holes into binary code.

Parallel: referring to the handling of data or instructions in groups of several bits rather than one bit at a time.

Peripheral device: any device that is used for input or output functions in conjunction with a computer.

Phototransistor: a device that generates electrical signals when exposed to light.

Pixel: short for picture element; one of the thousands of points on a computer screen from which digital images are formed.

Plotter: an output device that produces charts, graphs and other artwork in the form of line drawings on paper or film.

Polling: the process of testing each source of input in sequence to see if it has data ready, and each output port in sequence to see if it is ready to receive output.

Port: the connection between a computer and another device through which data enters and leaves.

Printer: an output device that prints computer results in numbers, letters or graphic images on paper.

Punched card: a rectangular card on which data is represented as punched holes.

Random-access memory (RAM): temporary internal memory whose contents can be altered by the CPU; sometimes called read and write memory.

Read: the process by which a computer's CPU examines data in memory or transfers data to memory from a storage medium such as a disk.

Read-only memory (ROM): permanent internal memory containing data or operating instructions that cannot be altered.

Real-time computing: computer processing rapid enough to solve problems and handle events as they occur.

Sampling: the process of taking the value of a signal at regular intervals, often used when converting analog signals, such as voltage, into digital ones.

Sensor: an information pickup device that converts physical energy such as temperature or light into electrical signals, which may then be translated for use by the computer.

Serial: pertaining to data that is processed in sequence, one bit at a time, rather than in groups of bits.

Software: instructions, or programs, designed to be carried out by a computer.

Standards: technical definitions accepted in computer science to ensure uniformity among devices and programs.

Stylus: a penlike input device that is used for drawing or writing on pressure-sensitive tablets.

Synthesizer: an electronic device for the production and control of sound.

Teletypewriter: a typewriter-like device capable of receiving or sending data in a communications system.

Terminal: a peripheral composed of a display or printing device and a keyboard, which are linked together to function as a single input/output unit.

Time sharing: the simultaneous use of a computer by more than one person.

Trackball: a ball, mounted and rotated in a box, used to direct the movement of a cursor on a display screen.

Transistor: an electronic semiconductor device used as a switch or an amplifier.

Voice recognition: the translation by a computer of spoken commands into digital instructions.

Window: a defined portion of a file displayed on a CRT.

Word processing: the use of a computer for creating, displaying, editing, storing and printing text.

Write: the process by which a computer records data in memory, external storage or display devices.

Bibliography

Books

Augarten, Stan, *Bit by Bit*. New York: Ticknor & Fields, 1984.

Bateman, Wayne, *Introduction to Computer Music*. New York: John Wiley & Sons, 1980.

Bates, William, *The Computer Cookbook*. Englewood Cliffs, N.J.: Prentice-Hall, 1983.

Boorstin, Daniel J., *The Americans: The Democratic Experience*. New York: Random House, 1973.

Chamberlin, Hal, *Musical Applications of Microprocessors*. Rochelle Park, N.J.: Hayden Book Company, 1980.

Considine, Douglas M., and Glenn D. Considine, eds., *Van Nostrand's Scientific Encyclopedia*. New York: Van Nostrand Reinhold, 1983.

Darter, Tom, comp., and Greg Armbruster, ed., *The Art of Electronic Music*. New York: Quill, 1985.

De Bono, Edward, *Eureka!* New York: Holt, Rinehart and Winston, 1974.

Edwards, Perry, and Bruce Broadwell, *Data Processing: Computers in Action*. Belmont, Calif.: Wadsworth, 1982.

Flores, Ivan, *Peripheral Devices*. Englewood Cliffs, N.J.: Prentice-Hall, 1973.

Glass, Robert L., *Computing Catastrophes*. Seattle: Computing Trends, 1983.

Hutchins, Carleen Maley, introduction to *The Physics of Music: Readings from Scientific American*. San Francisco: W. H. Freeman, 1978.

Laurie, Peter, *The Joy of Computers*. Boston: Little, Brown, 1983.

Levy, Steven, *Hackers: Heroes of the Computer Revolution*. Garden City, N.Y.: Doubleday, 1984.

Nichols, Elizabeth A., Joseph C. Nichols and Keith R. Musson, *Data Communications for Microcomputers*. New York: McGraw-Hill, 1982.

Osborne, Adam, and David Bunnell, *An Introduction to Microcomputers: Volume 0, The Beginner's Book*. Berkeley, Calif.: Osborne/McGraw-Hill, 1982.

Panata, Charles, *The Browser's Book of Beginnings*. Boston: Houghton Mifflin, 1984.

Pierce, John R., *The Science of Musical Sound*. New York: Scientific American Library, 1983.

Ralston, Anthony, and Edwin D. Reilly Jr., eds., *Encyclopedia of Computer Science and Engineering*. New York: Van Nostrand Reinhold, 1983.

Randell, Brian, ed., *The Origins of Digital Computers: Selected Papers.* New York: Springer-Verlag, 1982.

Redmond, Kent C., and Thomas M. Smith, *Project Whirlwind: The History of a Pioneer Computer.* Bedford, Mass.: Digital Press, 1980.

Roads, Curtis, and John Strawn, eds., *Foundations of Computer Music.* Cambridge, Mass.: M.I.T. Press, 1985.

Sadie, Stanley, ed., *The New Grove Dictionary of Music and Musicians.* London: Macmillan, 1980.

Shelly, Gary B., and Thomas J. Cashman, *Introduction to Computers and Data Processing.* Fullerton, Calif.: Anaheim Publishing, 1980.

Sobel, Robert, *I.B.M.: Colossus in Transition.* New York: Bantam, 1981.

Stern, Nancy, *From ENIAC to UNIVAC: An Appraisal of the Eckert-Mauchly Computers.* Bedford, Mass.: Digital Press, 1981.

Stevens, S. S., Fred Warshofsky and the Editors of Time-Life Books, *Sound and Hearing* (Life Science Library series). Alexandria, Va.: Time-Life Books, 1980.

Walker, Roger S., *Understanding Computer Science.* Fort Worth, Texas: Texas Instruments, 1981.

Wexelblat, Richard L., ed., *History of Programming Languages.* New York: Academic Press, 1981.

Zaks, Rodnay, and Austin Lesea, *Microprocessor Interfacing Techniques.* Berkeley, Calif.: Sybex, 1980.

Periodicals

Ahrens, Kristine A., "Word Processing: 50 Years in Retrospect." *The Office,* June 1982.

Annals of the History of Computing, October 1983.

Bashe, C. J., et al., "The Architecture of IBM's Early Computers." *IBM Journal of Research and Development,* September 1981.

Beattie, H. S., and R. A. Rahenkamp, "IBM Typewriter Innovation." *IBM Journal of Research and Development,* September 1981.

Becker, Joseph D., "Multilingual Word Processing." *Scientific American,* July 1984.

Bonn, Ted, "Developing UNIVAC's Plated Thin Film Metal Recording Tape." *The Computer Museum Report,* Fall 1983.

Brody, Herb, "Kurzweil's Keyboard." *High Technology,* February 1985.

Burks, Arthur W., and Alice R. Burks, "The ENIAC: First General-Purpose Electronic Computer." *Annals of the History of Computing,* October 1981.

Bylinsky, Gene:
"A New Industrial Revolution Is on the Way." *Fortune,* October 5, 1981.
"The Race to the Automatic Factory." *Fortune,* February 21, 1983.

Campbell-Kelly, Martin:
"Programming the EDSAC: Early Programming Activity at the University of Cambridge." *Annals of the History of Computing,* January 1980.
"Programming the Mark 1: Early Programming Activity at the University of Manchester." *Annals of the History of Computing,* April 1980.

Cowan, Les, "Joysticks and Trackballs Come of Age." *Popular Computing,* December 1983.

"Crashing through the Envelope." *Time,* September 10, 1984.

Cummings, Conrad, "An American at IRCAM." *High Fidelity,* August 1980.

"Designing Artificial Joints by Computer." *Technology Review,* October 1984.

"Grumman Begins X-29A Taxi Tests following Aircraft Rollout." *Aviation Week & Space Technology,* September 3, 1984.

Gunn, Thomas, "The Mechanization of Design and Manufacturing." *Scientific American,* September 1982.

Heppenheimer, T. A., "Chipmaster." *OMNI,* February 1985.

Hurd, Cuthbert C., "Early IBM Computers: Edited Testimony." *Annals of the History of Computing,* April 1981.

Kaplan, Gadi, ed., "The X-29: Is It Coming or Going?" *IEEE Spectrum,* June 1985.

Kley, Vic, "Pointing Device Communication." *Computer Graphics World,* November 1983.

Leibson, Steve:
"The Input/Output Primer, Part 1: What Is I/O?" *BYTE,* February 1982.
"The Input/Output Primer, Part 2: Interrupts and Direct Memory Access." *BYTE,* March 1982.
"The Input/Output Primer, Part 3: The Parallel and HPIB (IEEE-488) Interfaces." *BYTE,* April 1982.
"The Input/Output Primer, Part 4: The BCD and Serial Interfaces." *BYTE,* May 1982.
"The Input/Output Primer, Part 5: Character Codes." *BYTE,* June 1982.
"The Input/Output Primer, Part 6: Interrupts, Buffers, Grounds, and Signal Degradation." *BYTE,* July 1982.

Lu, Cary, "Computer Pointing Devices: Living with Mice." *High Technology,* January 1984.

May, F. T., "IBM Word Processing Developments." *IBM Journal of Research and Development,* September 1981.

Moorer, James Anderson, "Signal Processing Aspects of Computer Music: A Survey." *Proceedings of the IEEE,* August 1977.

PC, November 27, 1984.

PC, September 17, 1985.

"Plugged-In Prose." *Time,* August 10, 1981.

"Reaching for the Future." *Technologies Journal,* Vol. 4, No. 1, 1985.

Rich, Alan, "Composers with Computers." *Smithsonian,* December 1984.

Skalka, Patricia, "Someday I Will Walk Again." *Reader's Digest,* November 1983.

Snyder, Roger, "Ink Jet Printers." *Computers & Electronics,* April 1985.

Spector, Alfred, and David Gifford, "The Space Shuttle Primary Computer System." *Communications of the ACM,* September 1984.

Stern, Nancy, "The BINAC: A Case Study in the History of Technology." *Annals of the History of Computing,* July 1979.

Stevenson, Malcolm G., "Bell Labs: A Pioneer in Computing Technology." *Bell Laboratories Record,* 1974.

Taubes, Gary, "The Ultimate Theory of Everything." *Discover,* April 1985.

Tierney, John, "The Real Stuff." *Science,* September 1985.

Tucker, Jonathan B., "Making Music with Micros." *High Technology,* July 1984.

"Two Flat-Display Technologies." *BYTE,* March 1985.

Warwick, Graham, "Forward-Sweep Technology." *Flight Interna-*

tional, February 23, 1985.
"Winged Wonder." *Time,* September 10, 1984.

Other Publications
Dorfman, Nancy S., "New vs. Established Enterprises: A Study of Innovation in Computers and Semiconductors." Cambridge, Mass.: Center for Policy Alternatives, Massachusetts Institute of Technology, 1984.
Epson User's Manual: RX-80 Printer. Torrance, Calif.: Epson America, Inc., 1983.

The Home Computer Advanced Course. London: Orbis Publications, 1984.
The Home Computer Course. London: Orbis Publications, 1984.
Whitaker, A., and J. Chin, "X-29 Digital Flight Control System Design." Grumman Aerospace Corporation, Bethpage, N.Y.
X-29 Advanced Technology Demonstrator. Bethpage, N.Y.: Grumman Corporation, no date.
Yamaha International Corporation, *Digital Programmable Algorithm Synthesizer: Operation Manual.* Buena Park, Calif.: Yamaha International Corp., no date.

Acknowledgments

The index for this book was prepared by Mel Ingber. The editors also thank: **In France:** Paris—Eric Auffret, Computerland; Pascale Bernheim, IRCAM. **In Great Britain:** East Molesey, Surrey—Stephen Hobday, P.C.D.-Maltron Ltd. **In Japan:** Tokyo—Shigehiko Kikuchi; Kumiko Mogi; Akemi Oikawa; Oki Electric Industry Co. Ltd.; Tokyo Shibaura Electric Co. **In the United States:** California—Buena Park: Jim Smergel, Yamaha Music International; Camarillo: Charles Woznick, Techmedica, Inc.; Cupertino: Douglas Engelbart, McDonnell Douglas Information Systems Group; Los Angeles: Dr. Alan C. Kay, Apple Computer, Inc.; Milpitas: Mark Sherman, Atari Games Corp.; Moffett Field: Herb Vykukal, NASA Ames Research Center; Oakland: Vic Kley, KA Design Group; Palo Alto: Gloria Warner, Xerox PARC; Redwood City: James Ennis Kirkland, Woodside Design Associates; San Rafael: Perry S. Babb; Santa Clara: Steve Kirsch, Mouse Systems; District of Columbia—Rick Houk, Bono Film Services, Inc.; Robert Mikesh, Smithsonian Institution; Charles R. Redmond, NASA; John Williams, The Software Specialist; Idaho—Boise: Artie Stone, Hewlett-Packard Corporation; Illinois—Waukegan: Tom Giles, Cherry Electrical Products; Maryland—Clinton: Mark Krenik, Clinton Computer; College Park: William J. Allen Jr., Electronics Plus; Fort Washington: Frederick B. Maxwell and Kenneth A. Taschner, ADEC, Inc.; Wheaton: Bruce D. Monson, American Connections International, Inc.; Massachusetts—Boston: Oliver Strimpel and William Wisheart, The Computer Museum; Lexington: Douglas Ross; Lowell: Ed Pignone, Wang Industries; Michigan—Lansing: Martin King and Hugo Patterson, The Eyescan Company; New Hampshire—Amherst: Jack Gilmore; Greenville: Joseph H. Nestor; New Jersey—Princeton: Paul Lansky, Princeton University; New York—Bethpage: John Dannenhoffer, Michael Drake, Richard Kupczyk, Charles Sewall and Arnold Whittaker, Grumman Corporation; New York: Linda J. Errante, The Hospital for Special Surgery; Poughkeepsie: William P. Heising, IBM; Ohio—Cincinnati: Alan Ackenhausen and Eugene Merchant, Metcut Research Associates; Utah—Salt Lake City: Peter Doenges and John Briggs, Evans & Sutherland; Virginia—Alexandria: Kim Johnson and Sylvia Mabie, Clinton Computer; Arlington: Al Alawine and Ron Peay, Arlington Electronic Wholesalers, Inc.; Hampton: Skip Nunamaker, Langley Research Center; Washington—Bellevue: Greg Hickman and Min S. Yee, Microsoft Corp.; Wisconsin—Milwaukee: George Huhnke and Mary Hollrith, Johnson Controls. **In West Germany:** Munich—Rainer Gebauer, *CHIP* magazine; Stuttgart—Thomas Hartman, Daimler-Benz; West Berlin—Johannes Drosdol, Daimler-Benz.

Picture Credits

The sources for the illustrations that appear in this book are listed below. Credits from left to right are separated by semicolons, from top to bottom by dashes.
Cover, 6: Art by Matt McMullen. 10: Art by Walter Hilmers Jr. from HJ Commercial Art. 12, 13: Courtesy AT&T Bell Laboratories; courtesy The Computer Museum, Boston; courtesy J. V. Atanasoff, copied by Thomas E. Molesworth; courtesy The Computer Museum, Boston; MITRE Corporation(2); from *Automated Data Processing,* published by Moore Business Forms Inc., Niagara Falls, New York, courtesy Library of Congress except bar, art by Matt McMullen. 14, 15: Courtesy The Computer Museum, Boston; Bank of America Archives(2)—courtesy The Computer Museum, Boston; Lou Goodman(2); courtesy The Computer Museum, Boston, except bar, art by Matt McMullen. 19-33: Art by Matt McMullen. 36: Smithsonian Institution Photograph No. 30529. 40, 41: Art by Walter Hilmers Jr. from HJ Commercial Art, Maltron keyboard © P.C.D.-Maltron Ltd., East Molesey, Surrey, England. 44: Photographs, Oki Electric Industry Company Ltd., Tokyo—Andreas Dannenberg, courtesy Shibaura Electric Company, Tokyo—Oki Electric Industry Company Ltd., Tokyo. 47-59: Art by Sean Daly. 60: Fil Hunter. 63: Marvin Koner for *Fortune.* 65: Courtesy Douglas C. Engelbart. 66, 67: Jon Brenneis for *Fortune.* 68-71: Art by Sam Haltom from Another Color Inc. 72: Courtesy Dr. Alan C. Kay. 75: Courtesy Xerox Corporation. 76, 77: Derek Bayes/ASPECT, London. 79: Courtesy The Computer Museum, Boston. 80, 81: Screens by Laboratorium Frieder Michler, Lauterstein, West Germany, line art by Walter Hilmers Jr. from HJ Commercial Art; courtesy of Daimler-Benz AG, Stuttgart. 85: Paintings by Attila Hejja. 86-93: Paintings by Attila Hejja, line art by Walter Hilmers Jr. from HJ Commercial Art. 94, 95: © Alan Zenuk. 99: Courtesy The Eyescan Company, Lansing, Michigan—art by Roger Essley. 101: © 1984 Ted Streshinsky. 102, 103: Art by Pamela Lee. 104, 105: Art by Brian Sullivan. 106: John Goodman. 107: © Alan Zenuk. 108: Art by Harold Cohen, photographed by Becky Cohen—© 1980 art by David Em. 109: Lucasfilm Computer Graphics Division—art by Keith Haring. 111-121: Art by Roger Essley.

Index

Numerals in italics indicate an illustration of the subject mentioned.

A

Alto. *See* Xerox PARC
Analog-to-digital converters, 19, *20-23*, 113
Analytical Engine, 8-9
Apple Computer Company, 74; Apple II Plus, 95, 96; Lisa, 74; Macintosh, 75
ARC (Augmentation Research Center), 64, 66, 67
ARPA (Advanced Research Projects Agency), 64, 66, 67
ASCII (American Standard Code for Information Interchange), 45, 51
Assembly languages, 38
Atanasoff-Berry Computer, *12*
Atari Corporation, 74
Automation in manufacturing, 77-79

B

Babbage, Charles, 8-9
Babbitt, Milton, 100
Bell Laboratories, 11, 101, 106; Model I, 11, *12*
BINAC (Binary Automatic Computer), 15,
Binary arithmetic, 23
Boulez, Pierre, 106
Buses, 26-27

C

CAD (computer-aided design), 78
CAD/CAM, 78, 79
Cahill, Thaddeus, 98
Calvert, Thomas, 110
CAM (computer-aided manufacturing), 78, 79
Carlos, Walter, 101
Center for Computer Research in Music and Acoustics (CCRMA), 101, 106, 107
Centronics, 46
Character generator, *52*
Character recognition, 97-98
Choreography, computer-assisted, *94*, 95, *107*, 110
Chowning, John, 106, 110
Cohen, Harold, 108
Colossus, 11
Compatibility, 62; plug, 63
Complex Number Calculator (Model I). *See* Bell Laboratories
Computer, basic parts of, *26-27*
Computer art, *108-109*
Copland, Aaron, 101
Coupleux, Edouard E., 100
CPU (central processing unit), *26, 27, 28, 29, 30*

CRT (cathode-ray tube), 12, *13*, 18, 32, *54-55*; and word processor, 43
Cursor control, *68-71*

D

Daimler-Benz, driving simulator of, *80-81*
Data synchronizer, 18
Davis, Nan, 96-97
Deere & Co., 79
Deutsch, Herbert, 100
Diablo Systems, 45-46
Digital Equipment Corporation, 35-36
Digital FM, 106, 107, *118-119*
Digital-to-analog conversion, *32*, 117
Disabled, computer assistance for, 95-98, 99
DMA (direct-memory-access) controller, 26, *27, 30-31*
Dvorak, August, 41; keyboard, *41*
Dynabook, *72*, 73-74, 75

E

Eckert, J. Presper, 15-16
Editors, program, 38-39
EDSAC, 13, 38
EDVAC, 15
Em, David, 108
Engelbart, Douglas, 64, *65*, 66-67, 75
ENIAC, 11-12, *13*
Environmental regulation systems, 82
Epson Corporation, 46
ERMA (Electronic Recording Method of Accounting), *14*
Evans, Bob O., 62
Evans, David, 72
Eyescan Communicator, *99*

F

Fire detection, 82
Flat-panel display, *55*
Flex, 73
Flexowriter, 12, *13*, 35, 46
FMS (flexible manufacturing systems) 78-79
Forrester, Jay W., 12
Fourier, Jean Baptiste, 113

G

General Electric, 79
Gilmore, Jack, 38-39
Givelet, Joseph A., 100
Glidden, Carlos, 36
Graphics, image-generation, *53*
Grumman Aerospace Corporation X-29, 7, *85*, *86-93*; sensors, *88-89*, *90-91*

H

Hammond Organ, 100
Haring, Keith, 108
Hersey, John, 45

High-energy physics, 76, 77, 82
Hobday, Stephen, 41
Hollerith, Herman, 9, 10

I

IBM, 9, 46, 61; entry into computer production, 17-18; 701, *14*, 18; Stretch (7030), *15*; System/360 development, 61-63; typewriters, 42-43; XT, 96
Icons, 74
Interrupts, *28-29*; nonmaskable, 28
I/O controller, 26, 27, *28-29*
I/O technology, 7-8, *12-15*, 19, *20-33*
IRCAM (Institute for Research and Coordination of Acoustics and Music), 106
Itek Corporation, 15

J

Jacquard, Joseph Marie, 8
Japanese characters, *44-45*
Jobs, Steven, 74, 75
Joystick, *70-71*

K

Kay, Alan, 72-73, 75
Keyboards, 12, 13, 16, 47; arrangements of, *40-41*; interpretation of signals from, *50-51*; mechanisms, *48-49*
King, Martin, 99
Kotok, Alan, 36
Krum, Charles, 10
Krum, Howard, 10
Kurzweil, Raymond, 97-98, *106*, 107

L

Learson, T. Vincent, 61, *63*
Lexitron Corporation, 43
Light pen, *15*, 39
LOGO, 73
Lovelace, Ada, 8-9, 111
Lucasfilm, 108

M

McNabb, Michael, *101*
Magnetic cards, 43
Magnetic disk, 18, 43
Magnetic ink, *14*, 98
Magnetic tape, *14*, 16, 17, 18; and typewriter, 43
Malt, Lillian, 41
Manchester Mark I, 13, 15
Marince, Gary, 95, 96
Marince, Rob, 95-96
Masterson, Earl, 16-17
Mathews, Max, 101, 106, 110
Mauchly, John W., 15-16
Memory, RAM and ROM, *26-27*
MIDI (Musical Instrument Digital Interface), 107

Mill, Henry, 36
M.I.T. (Massachusetts Institute of Technology), 12, 35-36, 38-39, 79, 97, 98
Monitors, *54-55. See also* CRT
Moog, Robert, 100-101, 107
Mouse, 67, *68-69*
MUSIC, 101
Music, synthesized, 98, 100-101, 106-107, 111; additive and subtractive techniques, *114-117;* analog, 98, 100-101; digital, 101, 106-107; digital FM, 106, 107, *118-119;* and mathematical models of instruments, *120-121;* and sound characteristics, *112-117*

N
Northrop Aircraft Company, 16

O
Olsen, Kenneth, 36
Output buffer, 57

P
Page, Homer, 97
Papert, Seymour, 73
Paper tape, 10-11, 13, 15, 78, 100
Pattern recognition, 98
P.C.D. Maltron keyboard, *40-41*
PDP-1, 35-36
Petrofsky, Jerrold, 96-97
Pierce, John, 101
Piner, Stephen, 36
Pixel, 53
Plotter, *32-33*
Polling, *28-29*
Ports, parallel and serial, *24-25,* 27
Printers, *56-59;* buffer, *57;* daisy-wheel, 45-46, *56;* dot-matrix, 46, 56, *57-59;* high-speed, 16-17, 18; ink-jet, *58;* laser, 46,

59; and typewriters, 36, 42
Printers, ball-mechanism, *15*
Programming, manual, 11-12, *13, 25*
Prostheses, computer-aided design and manufacturing of, 77-78
Punched cards, 8-9, *10,* 11, *12,* 18

Q
QWERTY keyboard, *40-41*

R
RCA Synthesizer, 100
Reading Machine, 97-98
Real-time computing, 85
Remington Rand, 16, 17, 36-37

S
SAGE (Semi-Automatic Ground Environment), 13
Security systems, 82-83
Sensors, analog, 20-21
Sholes, Christopher Latham, 36, 37, 40
Simulator, driving, *80-81*
Smalltalk, 74, *75*
Smart buildings, 82
Sound, characteristics of, *112-113*
Spacecraft systems, shuttle, 83-84
Spacesuits, experimental, *102-105*
Stanford Research Institute (SRI), *14,* 64
Stibitz, George, 11
Sutherland, Ivan, 73

T
Taylor, Robert, 66, 72
Teletypewriter. *See* Keyboards
Telharmonium, 98, 100
Thumbwheel, *70*
Trackball, 70, *71*
Twain, Mark, 37
TX-0, 35, 38

TX-2, 39
Typewriters, *36-38,* 42-43

U
UNIPRINTER, 17
UNISERVO, 16
UNIVAC, *14,* 16, 17, 36
University of Manchester, 13
University of Pennsylvania, 11

V
Van Dam, Andries, 66
Voice-entry terminal, 95-96
Vydec Corporation, 43

W
Wang, An, 43
Wang Laboratories, 43, 45
Watson, Thomas J., Jr., 18, 61, 63
Whirlwind, 12, *13,* 38
Wilkes, Maurice, 13, 38
Williams, F. C., 13
Wonder, Stevie, 98
Word processing, 35-36, 43, 45; for ideographic languages, *44-45;* software, 45. *See also* Editors, program; Printers; Typewriters

X
Xerox PARC (Palo Alto Research Center), *67, 72,* 73-74, *75;* Alto, 74, *75;* graphics program, 66; Star 8010, 74
X-29. *See* Grumman Aerospace Corporation X-29

Y
Yamaha, 107

Z
Zuse, Konrad, 12

Time-Life Books Inc.
is a wholly owned subsidiary of
TIME INCORPORATED

FOUNDER: Henry R. Luce 1898-1967

Editor-in-Chief: Henry Anatole Grunwald
President: J. Richard Munro
Chairman of the Board: Ralph P. Davidson
Corporate Editor: Ray Cave
Group Vice President, Books: Reginald K. Brack Jr.
Vice President, Books: George Artandi

TIME-LIFE BOOKS INC.

EDITOR: George Constable
Executive Editor: George Daniels
Editorial General Manager: Neal Goff
Director of Design: Louis Klein
Director of Editorial Resources: Phyllis K. Wise
Editorial Board: Dale M. Brown, Roberta Conlan,
Ellen Phillips, Gerry Schremp, Donia Ann Steele,
Rosalind Stubenberg, Kit van Tulleken,
Henry Woodhead
Director of Research and Photography:
John Conrad Weiser

PRESIDENT: William J. Henry
Senior Vice President: Christopher T. Linen
Vice Presidents: Stephen L. Bair, Edward Brash,
Ralph J. Cuomo, Robert A. Ellis, John M. Fahey Jr.,
Juanita T. James, James L. Mercer, Wilhelm R. Saake,
Robert H. Smith, Paul R. Stewart, Leopoldo Toralballa

Editorial Operations
Copy Chief: Diane Ullius
Editorial Operations: Caroline A. Boubin (manager)
Production: Celia Beattie
Quality Control: James J. Cox (director)
Library: Louise D. Forstall

Correspondents: Elisabeth Kraemer-Singh (Bonn);
Dorothy Bacon (London); Miriam Hsia (New York);
Maria Vincenza Aloisi, Josephine du Brusle (Paris); Ann
Natanson (Rome). Valuable assistance was also
provided by: Clive Freeman (Bonn); Judy Aspinall and
Millicent Trowbridge (London); Carolyn Chubet (New
York); Dick Berry (Tokyo).

Library of Congress Cataloguing in Publication Data

Main entry under title:
Input/output.
   (Understanding computers)
   Bibliography: p.
   Includes index
   1. Computers. 2. Electronic data processing.
I. Time-Life Books.   II. Series.
QA76.I486 1986   004   85-28832
ISBN 0-8094-5666-4
ISBN 0-8094-5667-2 (lib. bdg.)

For information about any Time-Life book, please write:
Reader Information
541 North Fairbanks Court
Chicago, Illinois 60611

UNDERSTANDING COMPUTERS

SERIES DIRECTOR: Roberta Conlan

Editorial Staff for *Input/Output*
Designer: Robert K. Herndon
Associate Editors: Neil Kagan, Jeremy Ross (pictures)
Series Administrator: Rita Thievon Mullin
Researchers: *Text Editors:*
Esther Ferington   Thomas H. Flaherty Jr.
Elise Ritter Gibson   Peter Pocock
Sara Mark   *Writers:*
Fran Moshos   Patricia Daniels
Philip K. Polishook   Lydia Preston
Nancy C. Scott
Assistant Designer: Antonio Alcalá
Copy Coordinator: Anthony K. Pordes
Picture Coordinator: Renée DeSandies
Editorial Assistant: Miriam Newton Morrison

Special Contributors: Ronald H. Bailey, Sarah Brash,
Richard D. James, John I. Merritt, Charles C. Smith,
Robert S. Stokes (text); Susan S. Blair, Marlene
Zimmerman (research)

GENERAL CONSULTANT

ISABEL LIDA NIRENBERG has dealt with a wide range of
computer applications, from the analysis of data collect-
ed by the Pioneer space probes to the matching of children and families for adoption agencies. She works at the
Computer Center at the State University of New York at
Albany, and assists faculty and students there with microcomputer applications.

OTHER CONSULTANTS

GWEN BELL is the President of the Computer Museum in
Boston, Massachusetts.

CHRIS CHAFE is a cellist and a composer with an interest
in computer music. A research associate at Stanford University's Center for Computer Research in Music and
Acoustics, he has also worked at the Institute for Research
and Coordination of Acoustics and Music in Paris.

ADELE GOLDBERG is manager of the Systems Concepts
Laboratory at the Xerox Palo Alto Research Center in Palo
Alto, California. She is currently President of the Associ-
ation of Computing Machinery.

J.A.N. LEE is a Professor of Computer Science at Virginia
Polytechnic Institute. Active in the field of computers
since 1958, he has a special interest in its history.

JACKIE POTTS is President of Worldwide Interface Designers and Executive Vice President of the Office Automation Society International.